Richard Prince

Jokes & Cartoons

jrp|ringier

"I eat politics and I sleep politics, but I never <u>drink</u> politics."

BARBARA GLADSTONE GALLERY

99 Greene Street New York NY 10012

Tel 212 431-3334 Fax 212 966-9310

RICHARD PRINCE – JOKES

<u>Fireman pulling drunk out of a burning bed</u>: You darned fool, that'll teach you to smoke in bed.
<u>Drunk</u>: I wasn't smoking in bed, it was on fire when I laid down.

A traveling salesman stopped by a farmhouse and asked for a night's lodging.
   "We're all filled up," said the farmer, "but you can sleep with the little redheaded schoolteacher."
   "That's all right," said the traveling salesman,
"I'm a perfect gentleman."
   "Fine," said the farmer, "so is the little redheaded schoolteacher."

"Are you drinking again? Doesn't your health mean anything to you?"
"Yes, it means something to drink to."

I met my first girl, her name was Sally.
Was that a girl, was that a girl. That's what people
kept asking.

Two friends ran into each other at the door of a psychiatrist's office.
"Are you coming or going?" asked one.
The other replied, "If I knew, I wouldn't be here."

Did you here about the fellow who stopped a woman on Broadway and told her, "You're the first white woman I've seen in six months."
"Where've you been," she inquired, "darkest Africa?"
"Nope, selling silk in Florida."

I never had a penny to my name, so I changed my name.

"I eat politics and sleep politics, but I never <u>drink</u> politics."

I went to see a psychiatrist. He said, "Tell me everything." I did,
and now he's doing my act."

I've been married for thirty-four years and I'm still in love with
the same woman. If my wife ever finds out, she'll kill me.

Jewish man talking to his friends: "If I live, I'll see you
Tuesday. If I don't I'll see you Wednesday."

"My mother and father keep fighting. They rant and they rave and
they shout."
"Who is your father?" somebody asked.
"that's what they're fighting about."

Here's my life story. I came from a very poor family.
   They couldn't afford to have children, so our
   neighbor had me.

I met my first girl, her name was Sally. Was that a
   girl, was that a girl.
That's what people kept asking.

My father was never home, he was always away drinking
   booze. He saw a sign saying DRINK CANADA DRY. So
   he went up there.

The way he looks in the morning! He ran after the
   garbage man and said, "Am I too late for the garbage?"
He said, "No, jump in."

A traveling salesman's car broke down one evening on a
   lonely road and he asked at the only farmhouse in
   sight, "Can you put me up for the night?"
"I reckon I can," said the farmer, "But you'll have to
   share a room with my young son."
"How do you like that," gasped the salesman, "I'm in the
   wrong joke."

Two guys sitting at a bar: "If I have another drink,"
   the first said, "I'll begin to feel it."
The second confided: "If I have another drink, I won't
   care who feels it."

A little old lady walked up to a cop and said,
   "I was attacked."
The cop said, "When?"
She said, "Twenty years ago."
The cop said "What are you telling me now for?"
She said, "I don't know, once in a while I like to
   talk about it."

Man walking out of a house of questionable repute,
   muttered to himself,
"Man that's what I call a business.. You got it,
   you sell it, and you still got it."

My neighbor's wife cried to me: "It was driving me crazy,"
she said, "I don't know where he spent his evenings.
One night I went home, and there he was."

A pink elephant, a green kangaroo and two yellow
snakes strolled up to the bar.
   "You're here a little early, boys." said the bartender.
"He ain't here yet."

I'm always kidding about my wife says the
bartender. "Every time I introduce her to anybody
they say. "Are you kidding?"

The old man stood at the gates of the cemetery
and wept. A passer-by stopped to comfort him.
   "Why are you crying?" the latter asked softly.
   "My daughter is laying in there," explained the
weeping one. "Sometimes I wish she was dead."

A housewife selected three small tomatoes and was
told by the grocer they were 75 cents.
   "What!" she exclaimed, "75 cents for those small
tomatoes? Well, you can just take them!"
   "I can't lady," replied the unhappy grocer, "there's
a 95 cent cucumber there."

A couple is driving to Miami Beach in a brand new car. As they're
driving he puts his hand on her knee. She says "We're married now,
you can go a little farther"
So he went to Ft. Lauderdale.

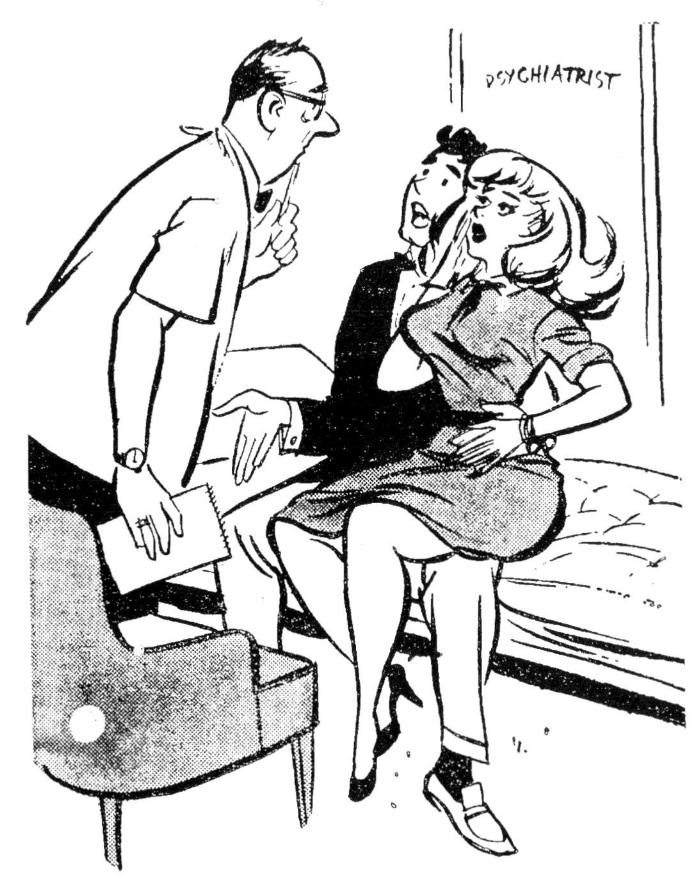
PSYCHIATRIST

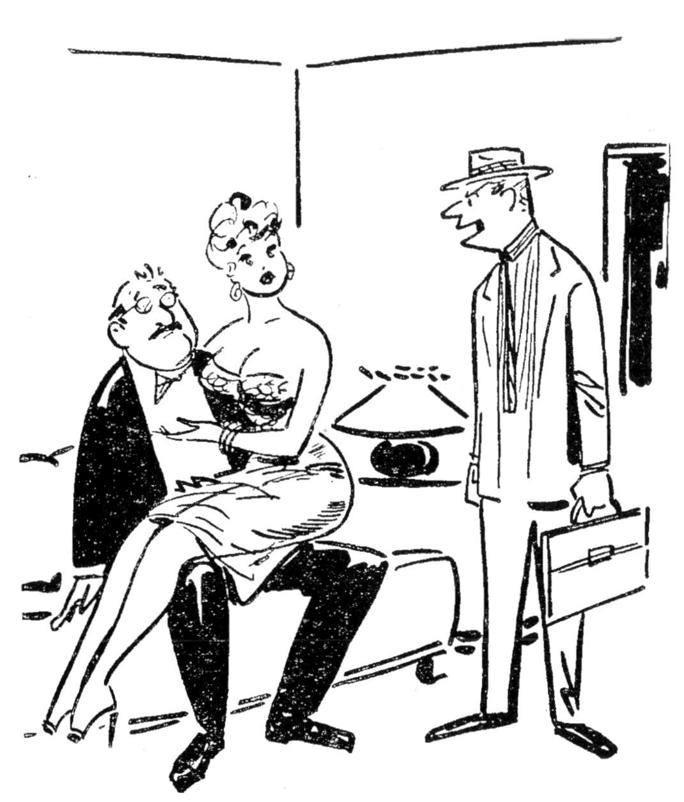

Two women are complaining about their boyfriends. One says to the other, "Oh God, here comes a delivery man with a bunch of roses. Christ, now I'll have to spend the entire weekend flat on my back with my legs spread in the air." The other woman says, "Why don't you just put them in a vase?"

Man walking out of a house of questionable repute, muttered to himself, "Man, that's what I call a business…you got it, you sell it, and you still got it."

Male Patient to Lady Psychiatrist: "I had a dream about you last nite." "Did you?" asked the Lady Doc. "No you wouldn't let me."

Two women are complaining about their boyfriends. One says to the other, "Oh God, here comes a delivery man with a bunch of roses. Christ, now I'll have to spend the entire weekend flat on my back with my legs spread in the air." The other woman says, "Why don't you just put them in a vase?"

Man walking out of a house of questionable repute, muttered to himself, "Man, that's what I call a business…you got it, you sell it, and you still got it."

Male Patient to Lady Psychiatrist: "I had a dream about you last nite." "Did you?" asked the Lady Doc. "No you wouldn't let me."

Two women are complaining about their boyfriends. One says to the other, "Oh God, here comes a delivery man with a bunch of roses. Christ, now I'll have to spend the entire weekend flat on my back with my legs spread in the air." The other woman says, "Why don't you just put them in a vase?"

Man walking out of a house of questionable repute, muttered to himself, "Man, that's what I call a business…you got it, you sell it, and you still got it."

Male Patient to Lady Psychiatrist: "I had a dream about you last nite." "Did you?" asked the Lady Doc. "No you wouldn't let me."

A guy goes into the doctor's office and says, "Hey doc I got five
penisis." The doc says "How do your pants fit?" The guy says,
"Like a glove."

A guy goes into the doctor's office and says,
"Hey doc I got five penisis."
The doc says "How do your pants fit?"
The guy says,"Like a glove."

Two psychiatrists, one says to the other
I was having lunch with my mother the
other day and I made a Freudian slip.
I meant to say please pass the butter
and it came out you fuckin bitch you
ruined my life.

George enterd a bar and ordered a whishky sour and told the bartender to fix the other guy at the bar a drink, too.
Finishing his first, he called to the bartender, "Fix me another of the same but leave the fruit out of it."
"Hey man!" shrieked the other guy, "I didn't ask for a drink in the first place!"

Later, as he sat on his balcony eating the dog...

Oh I rode into Dallas,
Feeling kinda low,
Thought I'd pick me up some change,
At the Ro-dee-o...

It is known that men and woman coming out jof an epileptic convulsion were inclined to be calmer and more peaceful for a time. So... if they were going to knock someone on the head to induce a seisure, they needed to use something more accurated than a hammer; they finally settled on electricity.

I'm so far underground, I get the bends.

Karl Marx's mother: "I wish Karl would accumilate money instead of writing about it."

Get it on. Bang a gong.

Eero Saacrinen's TWA terminal at LaGuardia.

"The retaliation", Robert Ginty, Sandahl Sigrid Thornton, brain surgery turns terrorist into killing machine.

One hour photo, drive thru burger, 0 to 60 mph in 6.00 sec., microwave cooking, personal 30 min. loans.

Trixie's delight.

Convulsions over homosexual acts and nude children.

The drummer Tommey Lee, dressed in a G-string and covered in tattoos, floated above the audience his drums on a platform moving to the far reaches of the stadium. The audience thrilled by his proximity went crazy and shouted even louder still.

Finding money is not a crive. crime.

The mother took her incorrigible son to the psychiatrist. "Does he seem to feel insecure?" asked the doctor, "No, the mother replied, "but everyone else in the neighborhood does."

Think of it as a turbo-charged TV.

I"m alright I guess.

Ever since they got married, the wife has had a padlocked chest by the foot of their
bed. Despite his pleading from time to time, she never revealed the contents to him.
Finally, on their silver wedding anniversary, the wife agreed to let him see the
contents. He watched steadfastly as she unlocked the chest and opened the lid.
Inside were two ears of corn and twenty five thousand dollars. He looked at the
chest and looked at his wife. His wife said, "its like this. Every time I cheated on
you, I put an ear of corn in." He was surprised to learn that she had been unfaithful.
But twice in twenty-five years wasn't that bad, so he smiled and asked, "what about
the money?" "Well, every time I reached a bushel, I sold it."

Marriage is grand.
Divorce is about ten grand.

How do you stop a Jewish girl from fucking?
You marry her.

What did Jesus say to the Mexicans?
Don't do anything until I get back.

I'm writing a new book that's going to have a field all to itself.
It's going to be for people who want to be unpopular, unsuccessful, and fat.

How can you tell your wife is dead?
The sex is the same but the dishes start to pile up.

She was so fat that when I had sex with her I had to ask for directions.
No No, that's not right - when I got to the top of her, my ears popped.

A father was explaining ethics to his son who was about to go into business:
"Supposing a woman comes in and orders $100 worth of materials. You wrap it up
And give it to her. She pays you with a $100 bill. As she goes out the door you realize
she has given you two $100 bills. Here's where the ethics come in, should you or
shouldn't you tell your partner?"

treezer.

His folks kept him in the closet for years.
Until he was fifteen, he thought he was a
suit.

My parents had a real strange attitude about me. You could call it queer.

My parents kept me in the closet for years. Until I was fifteen, I thought I was a suit.

BOY: I have forty cents. Do you think we could have a good time on that?
GRIL: I don't think so. My kid brother always gives me half a dollar.

My father was never home, he was always drinking booze.
He saw a sign saying **DRINK CANADA DRY**. So he went up there.

The way he looks in the morning!
He ran after the garbage man and said,
"Am I to late for the garbage?"
He said, "no, jump in."

A traveling sales man car broke down one evening on a lonely road and he asked at
the only farmhouse in sight, "can you put me up for the night?"
I reckon I can," said the farmer, "but you'll have to share a room the my young
son." "How about that," gasped the salesman, "I'm in the wrong joke."

<u>Two guys sitting at a bar</u>: "If I have another drink,"
 The first guy said, "I'll begin to feel it."
<u>The second confided:</u> "If I have another drink, I won't care who feels it"

A little old lady walked up to a cop and said, "I was attacked."
The cop said, "when?" she said, "twenty years ago."
The cop said," what are you telling me now for?"
She said," I don't know, once in a while I like to talk about it."

<u>Question</u>: Two men are in love with me, Murray and George.
 Who will be the lucky one?
<u>Answer</u>: Murray will marry you, George will be the lucky one.

Hers my life story. I came from a very poor family,
They couldn't afford to have children, so our neighbor had me.

In New Yorks Garment District a little old Jewish man was hit by a car. While waiting for an ambulance, the policeman tucked a blanket under the guy's chin and asked "Are you comfortable?" The man said, "I make a nice living!"

My mother was 88 years old. She never used glasses. Drank right out of the bottle.

Two dumb guys go bear hunting. They see a sign saying BEAR LEFT. So they went home.

A man goes to see a psychiatrist. The doctor says, "Your crazy." + the man says "I want a second opinion." "Okay, your ugly too!"

My wife, my wife. I took my wife to an Italian restaurant one nite. I asked her what she wanted. She said "the waiter."

I just sent my kid to real tough school. Christ the school newspaper has an obituary column.

I took my wife to a wife-swapping party. I had to throw in some cash

---

They asked one kid in school to prove the law of gravity. He threw the teacher out of the window

---

There's one guy that's really tough in our neighborhood. The other nite there was trouble. I saw him fire three warning shots INTO the guy he was warning!

I tell ya last week my wife made tomato surprise. Even the tomato was surprised.

94 x 96

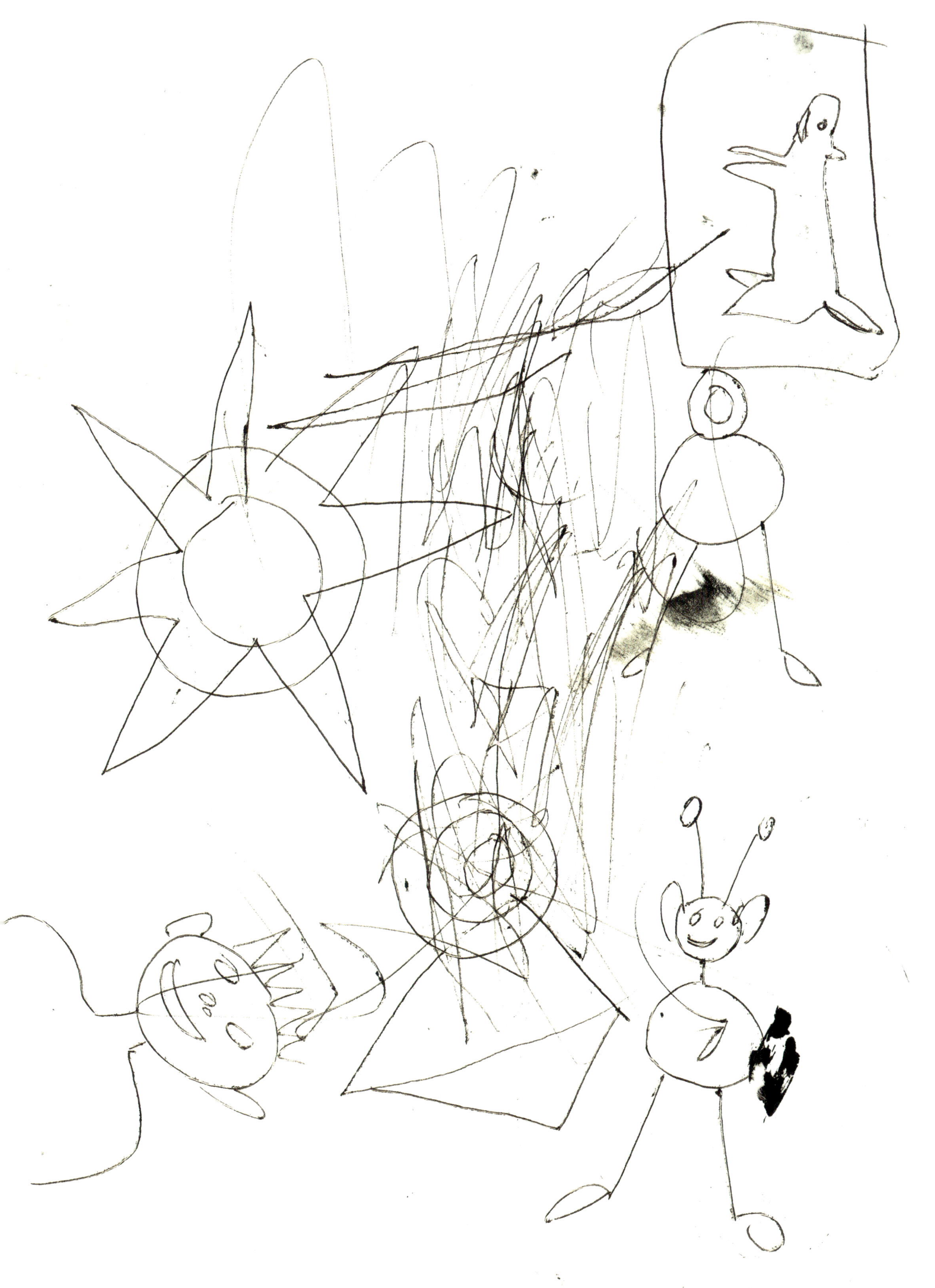

As was common, they got into a nasty quarrel at breakfast. "You're
not good in bed, either!" yelled the husband as he stormed out to
work. Around lunch time, he had cooled off and decided to apologize,
so he called home. After many rings, his wife answered. "What took
you so long?" he yelled as his temperate began to rise again.
"I was in bed."
"What were you doing in bed?"
"Getting a second opinion."

Ever since they got married, the wife has had a padlocked chest by
the foot of their bed. Despite his pleadings from time to time, she
never revealed the contents to him. Finally, on their silver
anniversary, the wife agreed to let him see the contents. He watched
steadfastly as she unlocked the chest and opened the lid. Inside
were two ears of corn and twenty-five thousand dollars. He looked at
the chest and looked at his wife. His wife said, "It is like this.
Every time I cheated on you, I put in an ear of corn." He was
surprised to learn she has been unfaithful. But twice in twenty-five
years wasn't that bad, so he smiled and asked, "What about the
money?" "Well, every time I reached a bushel, I sold it."

Both of my marriages have been disappointing. My first wife left me
and my second one didn't.

The husband bought his frigid wife a big tube of K-Y jelly and told
her, "This will make you happy." It did.
She put it on the bedroom doorknob after he went out.

Marriage is grand, divorce is about 10 grand.

I'm really clean
I put on a pair of clean socks on every day.
But at the end of the week I can't get my shoes on

I was in a generous mood Today, a woman says to her friend
I gave a poor beggar $25.
That's a lot of money says the friend - what did your husband
say. He said thank you.

what do you say to a one-legged hitchhiker
Hop in

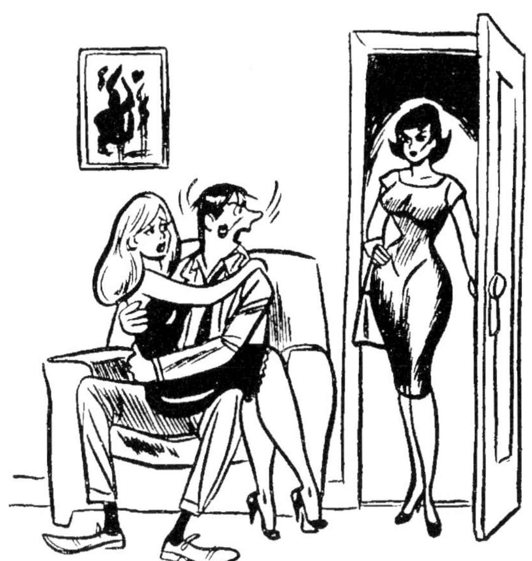

WITH MY WIFE I GOT NO SEX LIFE
SHE CUT ME DOWN TO ONCE A MONTH. BUT
HEY, I'M LUCKY. TWO GUYS SHE KNOWS
SHE CUT OUT COMPLETELY

My wife not to smart. The second time
she got pregnant she thought we had to get
married again.

My wife's not to smart. I told her sex life is
spoiled. She said don't worry that (if she)
spell like that.

You know me, & I love crowds?

You know me I can't things to relax last nite I went to a bar. I said
to the bartender surprise me. He showed me a naked
picture of my wife.

I'll tell ya I can't relax. I fe'

I'll tell my wife got no sex life
she cut me down to once a month. But hey I'm lucky
two guys she knows. She cut out completely

I'll tell ya with my wife we got no sex life
she

I'll tell ya I

I saw a man running out side my house naked
I said why are you naked. cause you came
home early.

I'll tell you I'm getting old
with me I wan't sex with two girls
or else I fall asleep then have
someone to talk to

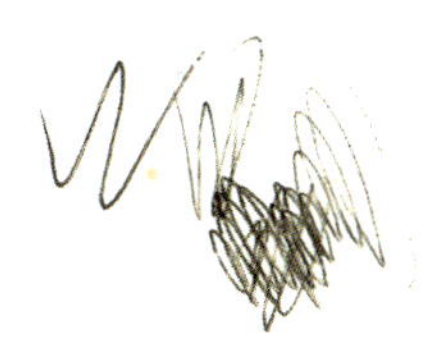

I collect rare photographs — I got one
~~with~~ where Norman Rockwell is beating up a child.

I got some powdered water but I don't know
what to add.

What's the difference between a penis and a bonus?
You can always get your wife to blow your bonus.

A guy ~~walks into a doctor's office~~ goes to a doctor and
says Doc I got a terrible case of discolored penis. Sure
enough the guy shows the Doc a bright blazin orangey penis.
The Doc never had seen anything quite like it and starts askin
about the guy's daily routine — any perscription medicin, did
he have more intercourse than average did he play any unusual
athletics — nope says the guy about the only thing I do
anymore is lay around, eat Cheetos and watch the Playboy
channel.

Both my marriages have been disappointing. My first wife
left me and my second one didn't.

Marriage is grand — Divorce is about 10 grand.
I put an ad in the classifieds: "Wife wanted". Next Day I got a hundred
replies. They all said the same thing: "You can have mine."

The mother took her incorrigible son to the psychiatrist. "Does he seem to feel insecure?" asked the
doctor. "No," the mother replied, "but everyone else
in the neighborhood does."

The faster you go.
Around the clock.
Anyone can find me.

I want to be your dog.

Krebs was killed in an accident.
And Silverman was sent to break the news to his wife.
"Be careful how ou tell her", advised a friend,
"She's a very delicate woman"
Silverman knocked on her door and she answered. "Pardon me,
are you the widow Krebs?"
"Certainly not".
"You wanna bet"?

A man was on safari with his native guide when they
came upon a beautiful blond bathing naked in the
steam. "My god, who's that?" the man asked.
  "Daughter of missinary, bwana," came the reply.
  "I havn't seen a white woman in so long,"
the man sighed "that I'd give anything to eat her."
  So the guide raised his rifle to his shoulder and ~~shot~~ *shot*
her.

Do you know what it means to come home at night to
a woman who'll give you a little love, a little affection,
a little tenderness? It means your're in the wrong house,
that's what it means.

A father was explaining ethics to his son who was
about to go into business: "Supposing a woman comes
in and orders $100 worth of material. You wrap it up and
give it to her. She pays you with a $100 bill. As she goes
out the door, you realize she has given you two $100
bills. Here's where the ethics come in. Should you or
shouldn't you tell your partner?"

George entered a bar and ordered a whisky sour
and told the bartender to fix the other guy at the
bar a drink, too.

Finishing his first, he called to the bartender,
"Fix me another of the same but leave the fruit
out of it." *Hey man!*
"~~Why, you wretch!~~" shrieked the other guy, "I
didn't ask for a drink in the first place!"

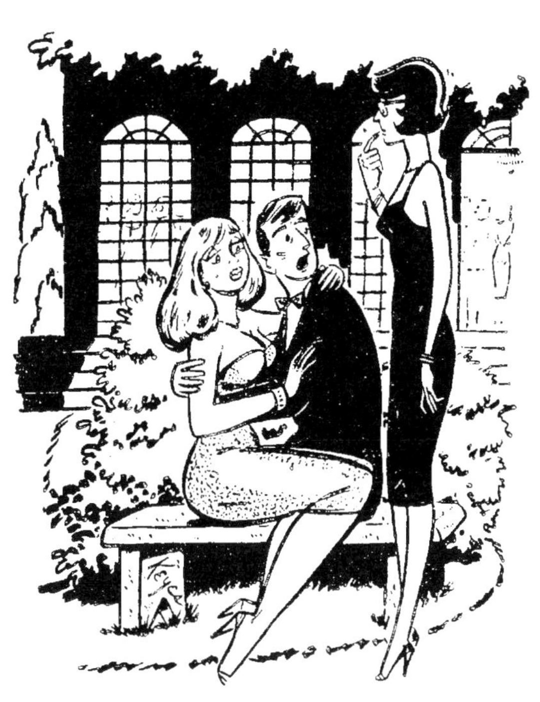

BARBARA GLADSTONE GALLERY

RICHARD PRINCE – JOKES
Page 2

RP214 My father was never home, he was always away drinking
booze. He saw a sign saying DRINK CANADA DRY. So
he went up there.

1986

RP215 The way she looks in the morning! He ran after the
garbage man and said, "Am I too late for the garbage?"
He said, "No, jump in."

RP216 A traveling salesman's car broke down one evening on
lonely road and he asked at the only farmhouse in
sight, "Can you put me up for the night?"
"I reckon I can," said the farmer, "but you'll have to
share a room with my young son."
"How about that," gasped the salesman, "I'm in the
wrong joke."

RP217 Two guys sitting at a bar: "If I have another drink,"
the first said, "I'll begin to feel it."
The second confided: "If I have another drink, I won't
care who feels it."

RP218 A little old lady walked up to a cop and said,
."I was attacked."
The cop said, "When?"
She said, "Twenty years ago."
The cop said, "What are you telling me now for?"
She said, "I don't know, once in a while I like to
talk about it."

3   40 × 28
3   70 × 50
1   48 × 70
2   80 × 47

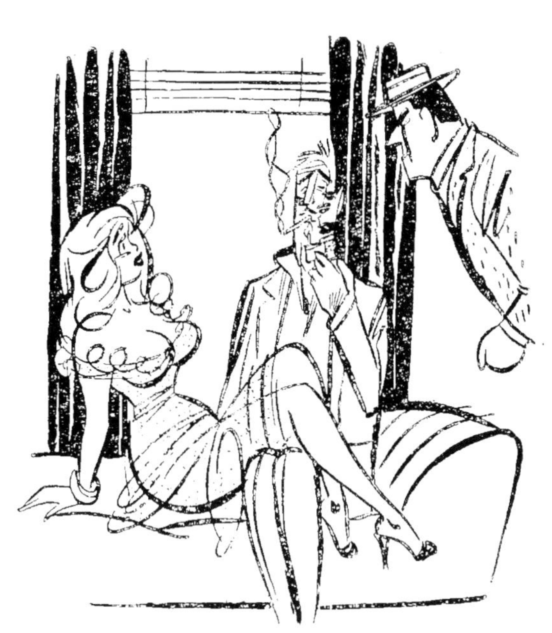

PRINCE

116

Split in Middle

Cut

Question: Two men are in love with me, Murray and George. Who will be the lucky one?
Answer: Murray will marry you. George will be the lucky one.

I've been normal for 34 years and I'm still in love with the same woman. If my wife ever finds out, she'll kill me.

Here's my life story. I come from a very poor family. They couldn't afford to have children, so our neighbors had me.

Two little Hollywood boys were exchanging taunts. "My father can beat your father." "Oh yeah? My father is your father."

I met my first girl, her name was Sally. Was that a girl—was that a girl. That's what people kept asking.

I went to see a psychiatrist. He said, "Tell me everything." I did, and now he's doing my act.

The way he looks in the morning! He ran after the garbage man and said, "Am I too late for the garbage?" He said, "No, jump in."

The ideal wife would be a beautiful, sex-starved deaf mute who owns a liquor store.

White man: "I don't know what to do. My house has burned to the
ground, my wife died, my car's been stolen, and the doctor says I
gotta have a serious operation."
Black man: "What you kickin' about, you white ain't you?"

A russian man saves up enough money to buy a new refrigerator. He
goes to the appropriate office and hands over the money.
"Your refrigerator," the official tells him, "will be delivered
exactly ten years from today."
"In the morning or in the afternoon?" the man asks.
"Why do you need to know that now?" the official asks.
"Because the plumber promised to come in the morning."

An American, a Pole, a Chinaman, and an Israeli are standing on a
street corner when a man comes over with a clipboard.
"Excuse me," he says "I am taking a poll. What is your opinion
of the meat shortage?"
The American asks: "What's a 'shortage'?"
The Pole asks: "What's 'meat'?"
The Chinaman asks: "Whats an 'opinion'?"
The Israeli asks: "What's 'excuse me'?"

I grew up to have my father's looks, my father's speech patterns,
my father's posture, my father's opinions and my mother's
contempt for my father.

How do we know Jesus was Jewish?
Four reasons:
1. He was thirty, unmarried, and still living with his mother.
2. He went into his father's business.
3. He thought his mother was a virgin.
4. And his mother thought he was God.

A mother is having a very tense relationship with her fourteen
year old son. Screaming and fighting are constantly going on in
the house. She finally brings him to a psychoanalyst. After two
sessions, the doctor calls the mother into his office.
"Your son," he tells her, "has an Oedipus complex."
"Oedipus, Scmedipus," the woman answers. "As long as he loves his
mother."

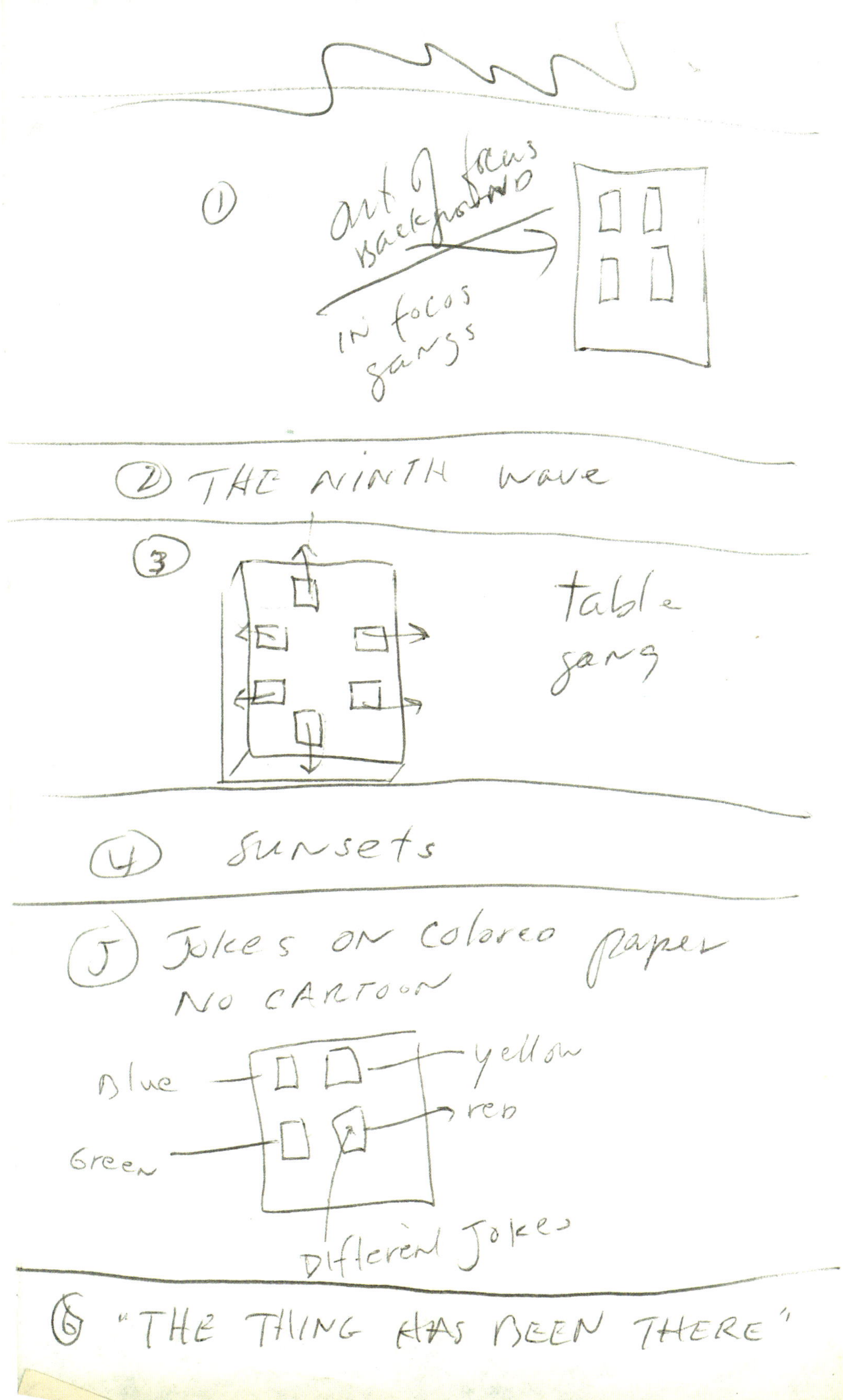

1) art of focus Backgound
in focus gangs

2) THE NINTH WAVE

3) table gang

4) sunsets

5) Jokes on colored paper
NO CARTOON
Blue
Green
yellow
red
Different Jokes

6) "THE THING HAS BEEN THERE"

Jacopo Robusti, better known as Tinteretto. (1518-94)

Evocative atmosphere, Arcadian poetry, mystery, music, and melancholy, captivating color, revolutionary churches by Giorgione at Venice.

Two cannibals were eating a clown when one turned to the other and said, " Does he taste funny to you?"

Man as animal is violent but as spirit is non-violent. The moment he awakens to the spirit within, he cannot remain violent. Either he progresses towards ahima, (non-violence) or rushes to his doom.

So many reactions to things are based on your mood.

I never had a penny to my name, so I changed my name.

Nancy to her girlfriend: "He said he was interested in humiliation, so I stood him up."

"I'm always kidding about my wife," says the bartender. "Every time I introduce her to anybody, they say, 'Are you kidding?'"

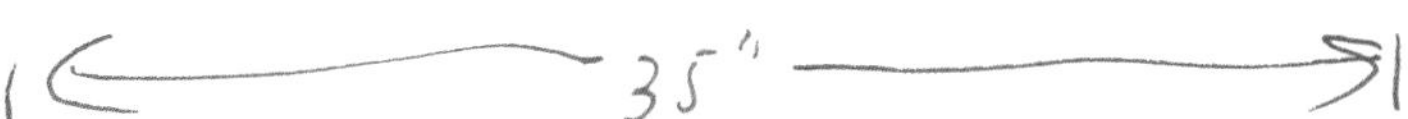

A long-haired hippie was hitchhiking when a
trucker picked him up. Heading down the road,
the hippie says to the trucker, "Bet you
thought I was a girl."
Replies the trucker, "Don't matter much, was
gonna fuck ya anyway."

PRINCE

I know a guy who took out a million dollar life insurance policy. He died anyway.

"My Parents kept me in a closet for years. Until I was fifteen I thought I was a su

"My brother just married a two-headed lady." "Is she pretty you ask?" "Well, yes and no."

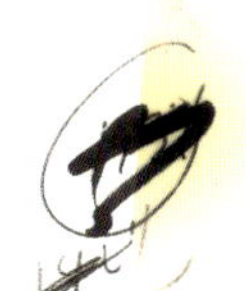

Last night I ordered a whole meal in French.
Even the waiter was surprised. I was
in a Chinese restaurant.

I went down to Miami. They told me to get
a lovely room for seven dollars a night. The room
was in Savannah, Georgia.

I went to the Doctor with a sore foot.
He said I'll have you walking within the hour.
He did. He stole my car.

The way things are going, I feel like a fool buying
a five year calender.

Im writing a new book thats gonna have a field all to itself.
Its for people who want to be unpopular, unsuccessful and fat.

Ladies and Gentlemen.
A funny thing happened to me while coming out to the
Microphone. I forgot my act.

I wont say what she does for a living but they
threw her out of one hotel cause she didnt have
a permit for a parade.

I once gave my girlfriend an old swimming suit, with
the covered knees and long skirt and made out of corduroy.
She was just delighted with it, laughing, skipping, running
around whirring up a storm - Then she jumped in the water
and we never saw her again.

I wont say shes fat, but who else has trouble
getting into a bathrobe.

Ricks Bisexual, any time he wants he has to
buy it.

Un camionneur effondre se presente a la gendar
merie:

Vous avez des vaches noires dans le pays?
Non!
Et des gros chiens noirs?
Non!
Alors, j'ai ecrase le cure...

A Montgomery, dans L'Alabama, la police vient
d'arreter un Noir pour port d'armes. Il avait
un couteau dans le dos...

Cheri, dis-moi ce que tu preferes. Une femme
jolie on une femme intelligente?
Ni l'unne, ni l'autre, cherie! Tu sais bien que je
n'aime que toi.

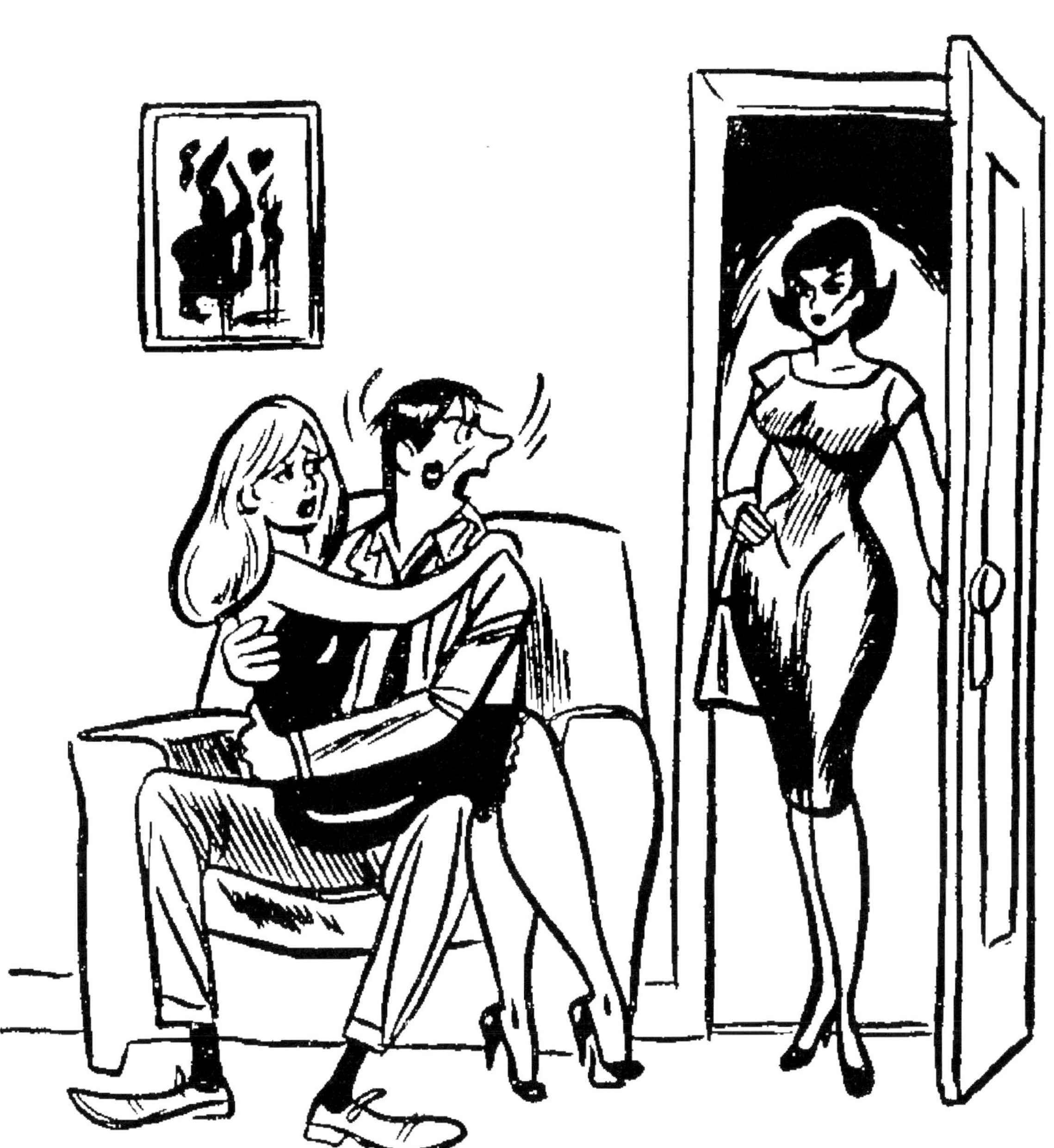

Dear Dick —

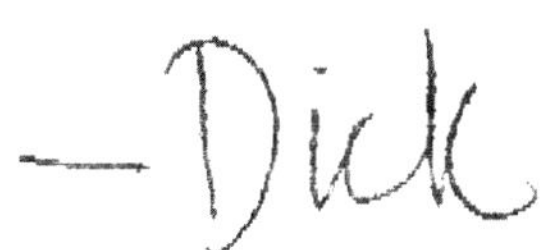

* So, I was talking to Charlie Manson
up there in prison the other day and
he says to me, "Is it hot in here
or am I crazy?"

So, I was talking to Charlie Manson the other day...
you know he's been up there in prison
for the last 20 years and he says to me,
"Is it hot in here or am I crazy?"

So, I was talking to Charlie Manson up in the prison
the other day and he says to me, "Is it hot
in here or am I crazy?"

* Please note:
The comma after so is optional. It depends on
whether or not you want a pause or a run.

For the record, the second version seems really clumsy
with the structure and the ellipse. My opinion solely .

—Dick

Male Patient to Lady Psychiatrist: "I had a dream about you last nite." "Did you?" asked the Lady Doc. "No you wouldn't let me."

A guy has a new dog. This dog he falls in love with.
The dog falls in love with his guy. Their crazy about each other.

each other. Then this guy wins a free trip to Paris. So he.
to Paris. So he leaves he dog with his sister. Good and bad.
Good and bad. What can he do?
     Two weeks later he calls the sister from Paris.
Over the phone he says, "How's my dog?"
     The sister say's, "Your dog died".
     He says, "Why did you tell it to me that way? You could
You could have told me the dog was on the roof, fell off,
fell off, broke his leg... you know, you could have told me
have told me gradually"
     The sister says, "I'm sorry".
     "O.K., I forgive you", the guy says. "By the
the way, how is Mom?.
     "She's on the roof".

I had a dream all ______ is of the pill came back- man were they
mad.

I accidently shot my mother in law while deer hunting. It was an
honest mistake. I came out of the tent in the morning and thought I
saw a deer in an orange vest making coffee.

A beautiful woman moved in next door. So I went and returned a
cup of sugar. She said you didn't borrow this.

A guy goes to the dentist sits in the chair, pulls down his zipper and
takes out his dick.
The dentist says what are you doing? I'm a dentist.
The guy says yeah, but there's a tooth in there.

I always know when my sister is having her period. Because my
father's prick tastes funny.

A horse walks into a bar. The bartender asks,"Hey buddy why the
long face?"

Doctor gives laxative to Mr Jay- one pill every four hours. Mr Jay
gets confused and takes four pills every hour.
Next morning his son yells,"Ma! Pop's dead in the bathroom!"
She yells back "I know, I'll call the undertaker as soon as he stops
shitting!"

Old guy sitting on a bus when a punk rocker gets on. The rocker's
hair is green and red, he's got feather earrings and an eye patch and
sees the old guy staring at him. He says.."What's the matter old man,
didn't you ever do anything wild?" The old guy says- "Yeah, on time
I fucked a parrot..I thought maybe you were my kid."

My boyfriend just married a girl who's bisexual.
Claims he's going to change her. He did.
Three years later she's a lesbian.

Very strange. The other day I saw a man with a wooden leg and a
real foot.

I have a circular driveway. Problem is I can't get out.

So I was talking to Charlie Manson
up there in prison the other day and
he says to me "is it hot in here
or am I crazy."

So I was talking to Charlie Manson the other day...
you know he's been up there in prison
for the last 20 years and he say's to me
"~~am I crazy or~~ "is it hot in here, or am I crazy?"

So I was talking to Charlie Manson up in the prison
the other day and he says to me "is it hot
in here or am I crazy."

Two cannibals were eating a clown when one turned to the other and said, "Does he taste funny to you."

My boyfriend just married a girl who was bi-sexual. Claimed he was going to change her. He did. Three years later she's a lesbian.

My parents kept me in a closet for years. Until I was fifteen I thought I was a suit.

I put an ad in a swinger's magazine and my parents answered it.

I had a dream all the ~~victims~~ victims of the pill came back — man they were mad.

A horse walks into a bar. The bartender says "Hey buddy why the long face"?

Hey thanks very much

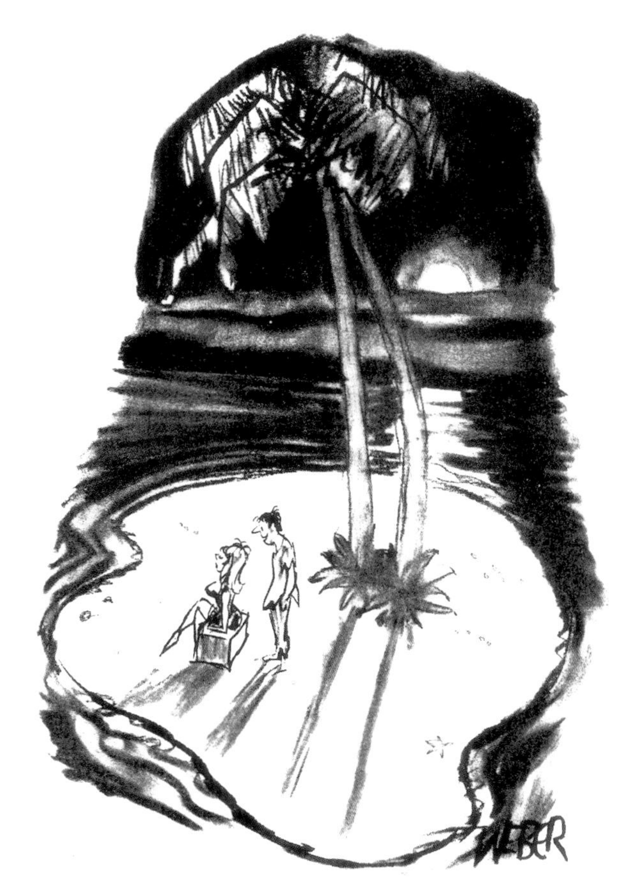

4 times the size

TWO GAY GUYS PISSING
IN A PUBLIC BATHROOM
WHEN ONE LOOKS OVER &
SEES THE OTHER WEARING
A NICOTINE PATCH ON HIS
PENIS. THE GUY SAYS
HEY WHAT'S THAT FOR

well
other
THE GUN says I've
CUT DOWN
to two BUTTS
A DAY.

with the patch

Man walking out of a house of questionable repute, muttered to himself, "Man, that's what I call a business…you got it, you sell it, and you still got it."

I had a friend who was a clown.
When he died all his friends went to his funeral in one car.

I pick up hitchhikers. When they get in the car I say fasten your seat belts.
I want to try something I once saw in a cartoon, but I think I can do it.

One night a jetliner flew a little to close to my house.
I was walking from the living room to the kitchen and the
Stewardess told me to sit down.

There's a fine line between fishing and standing on the shore looking like an idiot.

When I was five my father told me never to talk to strangers.
We haven't spoken since.

A guy gets a phone call from his doctor, who says, "I've got bad news and worse
news. The bad news is you've got 24 hours to live." "Good god!" says the guy,
"what's the worse news?" the doctor says "I've been calling you since yesterday."

A man was on safari with his native guide when they came upon a beautiful blond
bathing naked in the stream. "My god, who's that?" the man asked.
"Daughter of missionary, Bwana," came the reply.
"I haven't seen a white woman in so long," the man sighed,
"That I'd give anything to eat her." So the guide raised his rifle to his shoulder and
shot her.

Do you know what it means to come home at night to a woman who'll give you a
little love, a little affection, a little tenderness? It means you're in the wrong house,
that's what it means.

I have a circular driveway. Problem is I can't get out.

with all I've heard about
A-bombs that'll destroy a city
and H-bombs that'll destroy a
state and chain reactions that'll
destroy the world — you know
I just don't have the INCENTIVE
to buy a two pants suit.

Very strange, the other day I saw a man
with a wooden leg and a real foot.

I have a circular drive-way.
Problem is I can't get out.

I pick up hitch-hikers when they get in the car I say
fasten your seatbelts. I want to try something
I once saw it in a cartoon, but I think I
can do it.

one nite a jet liner flew a little to close to my house.
I was walking from the living room to the kitchen
and the stewardess told me to sit down.

I had a friend who was a clown. when he died
all his friends went to his funeral in one car.

There's a fine line between fishing and standing
on the shore and looking like an idiot.

When I was Ten my father told me never talk
to strangers. We haven't spoken since.
I was going to commit suicide by drowning; but I must not
have been serious because I brought a beach towel.

I like my new neighborhood. The Ice-cream truck plays Helter, Skelter
I broke my arm trying to fold a bed. It wasn't the kind that folds.

"I eat politics and I sleep politics, but I never drink politics."

The way she looks in the morning! She ran after the garbage man and said, "Am I too late for the garbage?" He said, "No, jump in."

I went to see a psychiatrist. He said, "Tell me." I did, and now he's doing my act.

"He asked me about some of my lovers. That didn't bother me, and I asked him about some of his lovers. What *did* bother me was that some of my lovers were some of his lovers."

"He asked me about some of my lovers. That didn't bother me, and I asked him about some of his lovers. What *did* bother me was that some of my lovers were some of his lovers."

"He asked me about some of my lovers. That didn't bother me, and I asked him about some of his lovers. What *did* bother me was that some of my lovers were some of his lovers."

"He asked me about some of my lovers. That didn't bother me, and I asked him about some of his lovers. What *did* bother me was that some of my lovers were some of his lovers."

I took another girl home…I told her I'd like to see what her apartment looked like. She drew me a sketch.

A horse walks into a bar. The bartender asks, "hey buddy why the long face?" "Doctor, my husband limps because his left leg is an inch shorter then his right leg. What would you do in his case?" "Probably limp"

"Doctor, my husband limps becuase his left leg is an inch shorter than his right leg. What do in his case?"

"Probably limp"

I went to the Doctor with a sore foot.
He said I'll have you walking within the hour.
He did. He stole my car.

The way things are going, I feel like a fool buying
a five year calendar.

I'm writing a new book that's gonna have a field all to itself.
It's for people who want to be unpopular, unsuccessful and fat.

Ladies and Gentlemen.
A funny thing happened to me while coming out to the
Microphone. I forgot my act.

I won't say what she does for a living but they
threw her out of one hotel cause she didn't have
a permit for a parade.

Last night I ordered a whole meal in French.
Even the waiter was surprised. I was
in a Chinese restaurant.

I went down to Miami. They told me I'd get
a lovely room for seven dollars a week. The room
was in Savannah, Georgia.

Sex between two people is beautiful.
Sex between five people is fantastic.

A guy falls out the window of a
twenty-story building. As he passes the
fourteenth floor a friend yells, "Hey Mike,
how's it going?"

You know I was up there in prison
talking to Charlie Manson and he says to
me, he says, "Is it hot in here or am I
crazy?"

Last night I ordered a whole meal in French.
Even the waiter was surprised. I was
in a Chinese restaurant.

I went down to Miami. They told me I'd get
a lovely room for seven dollars a week. The room
was in Savannah, Georgia.

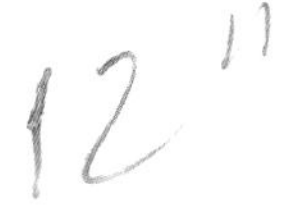

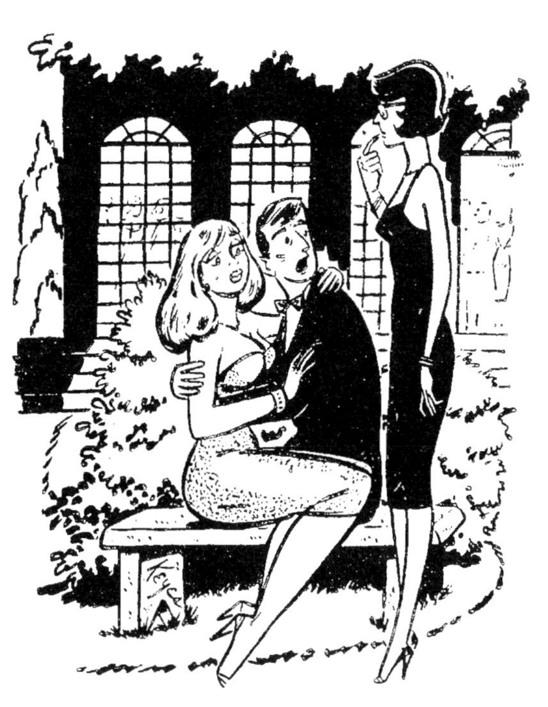

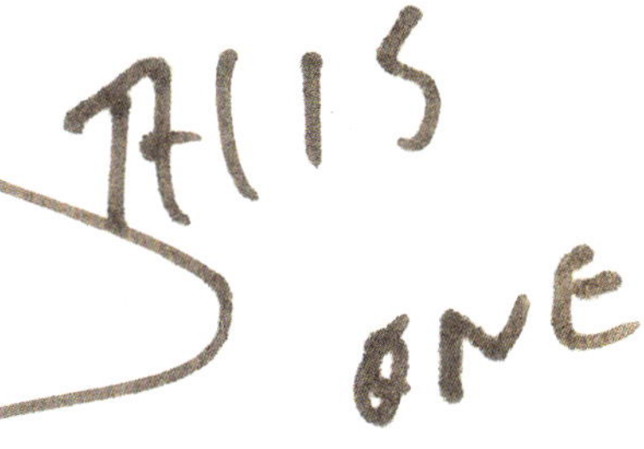

3

You know, I was up there in prison talking to Charlie Manson
And he says to me, he says, " Is it hot in here or am I crazy?"

Did an Italian crane operator just experience uninhibited sensations in a Malibu hot tub?

So if a couple from Kentucky get divorced, they are still brother and sister?

Why do Arabs stink? So blind people can hate them too.

So this is what it feels like to be potato salad.

My polyvinyl cowboy wallet was made in Hong Kong by Montgomery Clift.

Who sees a beach bunny sobbing on a shag rug.

What's the difference between kinky and erotic?
With kinky you use the whole chicken.

While in bed the husband reached over and started to fondle his wife's pussy.
 He did this for just a short while and then stopped and went back to his book.
Then the wife said, "hey, how come you stopped?" "Stopped what?" the husband
replied. "Stopped playing with my pussy." "Oh" sad the husband, "I was just
wetting my fingers to turn the pages of my book."

My mother and father keep fighting.
They rant and they rave and they shout.
"Who is your father?" somebody asked.
"That's what they're fighting about".

1) "Heck no, We're not crazy! Why? Do we look crazy?

2) "I've never felt such an absence of pain

3) It's a grand old flag.

4) But mommy I don't want to take a nap.

5) Ending his own life now? Are you kidding?
That's not his own life."

6) "No Thank you. I don't drink.

7) Did you catch that?
No. I talked him into giving himself up.
No I was sitting here minding my own business
when the crazy thing jumped into my pail.
No, its a plastic morsel to get people like
you to start fascinating conversations

8) "Let me ask you this. In the game Farmer and the Dell,
for instance, were you frequently the cheese left standing
alone?

9) I Roamed the world to find myself, and then I came home
and discovered happiness right here in my own back yard.

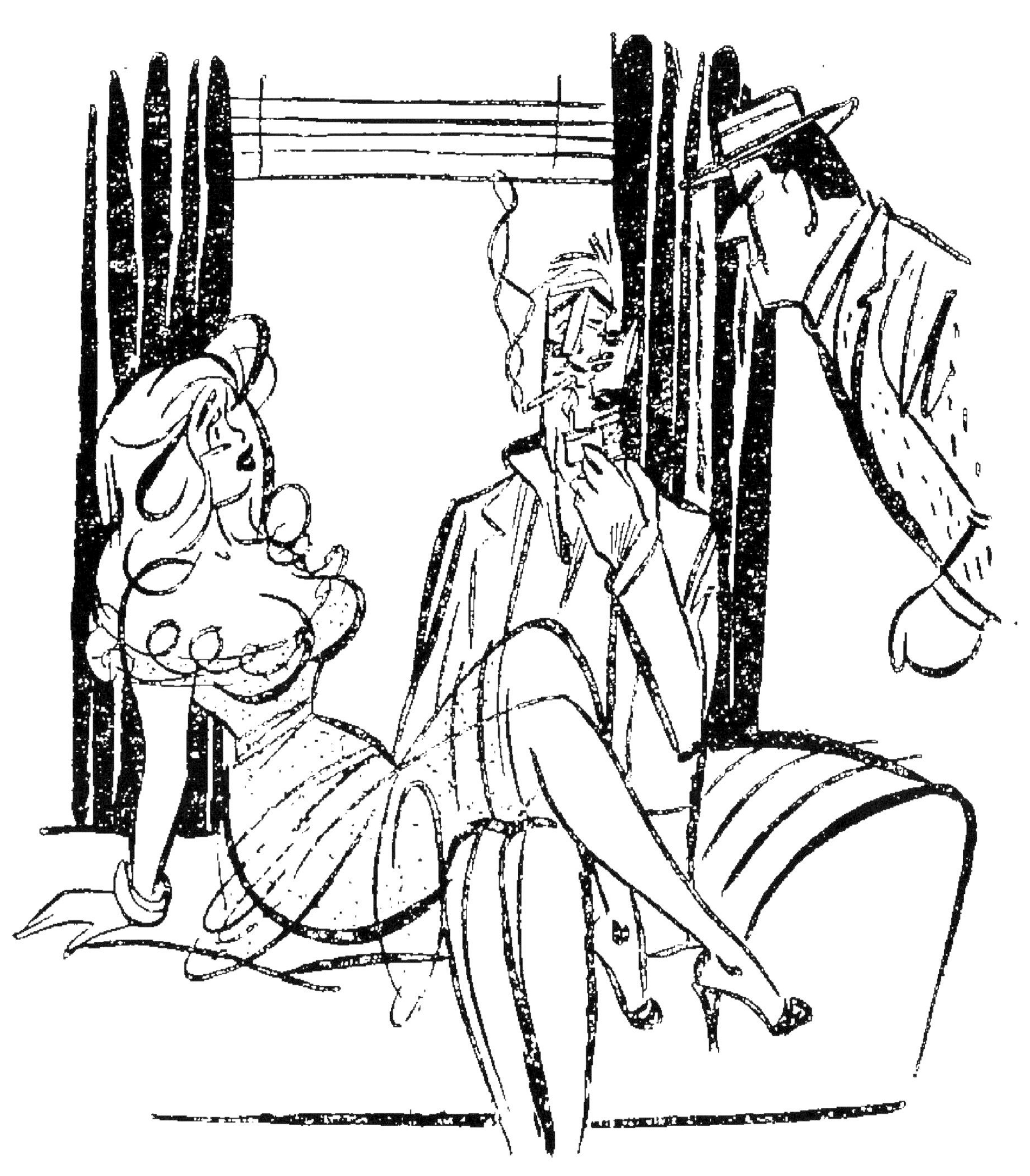

RICHARD PRINCE – JOKES
Page 3

1987

RP 219 "Are you drinking again? Doesn't your health mean
         anything to you?"
        "Yes, it means something to drink to."

RP 220 Did you hear about the fellow who stopped a woman on
         Broadway and told her, "You're the first white
         woman I've seen in six months."
        "Where've you been," she inquired, "darkest Africa?"
        "Nope, selling silk in Florida."

RP 221 Two friends ran into each other at the door of a
         psychiatrist's office.
        "Are you coming or going?" said one.
        The other replied, "If I knew, I wouldn't be here."

RP 222 Man walking out of a house of questionable repute,
         muttered to himself,
        "Man that's what I call a business ... You got it,
         you sell it, and you still got it."

99 GREENE ST

NEW YORK 10012

212 431 3334

73 : A general in tears is tenderly holding the hand of his wife who is about to die.
And she tells him :
-Darling, I cannot leave without telling you the truth. You have to know that I
have been unfaithful to you since we got married. But only twice. First with your
aide-de-camp and then with the 23rd regiment of artillery.

137 : In the States most of the teachers says that one should not be contradicted children.
It victimizes children. If your child wants to throw himself through the window
let him do it. Anyway he will not do it again.

142 : In Montgomery, Alabama, the police just caught a black man for prohibited
carrying of arms. He had a knife in his back. (stuck)

151 : Tell me darling who you prefer : a pretty woman or an intelligent
woman? Neither of them dear! You know that it's you that I only love.

160 : Nobody has ever wondered why girls look down when boys make a declaration
of love... Well just to know if they are telling the truth....

166 : In the middle of the creation of the world God calls an angel and scolds
him :
-Look what you have done ! he says pointing at a sole fish . I told
you to wash it not to iron it.

242 : Say Mummy , what is a vampire ?
Shut your mouth and drink up before it coagulates....

170: English cooking ? If it is hot it is soup . If it is cold it is beer;

184 : Two English boys are sitting in front of a soup tureen . the first one
tells the other :
- It is an iinteresting soup , not a great soup.

220 : A liner just sank . The head of an English Lord emerges from the water
and his hand grasps a providetial wreck , with his other hand he caresses
his chin :
- Let's see ... Let's see... Where was I ? Ah yes ...Help!

228 : An American multimillionaire is dying . Since he does not have any child
he calls his secretary to his bed :
- Liz , I have decided to leave you all my money
- Oh Sir , it is really kind of you ! What can I do to alleviate your
last moments
- Well , take your foot off the oxygene pipe !

1500: A man goes to the doctor and says :
" Doctor, I think I am impotent !
- Let's see that right now, says the doctor, show me your genitals !
And the man bites his tongue out _ _ _

05 :
    _ Dad what is in this tree?
    _ Black prunes
    _ But Dad they are not black they white
    _Yes . THey are white because they are still green.

06 :
    A man opens the newspaper and reads:
    In Chicago 20 times a day a man is shot down
 The reader nods his head and says:
    _ Poor guy !

09 :
    _ I am very worried all day long I see black spots
    _ Did you see an ophtalmologist?
    _ No, not an ophtalmologist, black spots.

17:
    A car driver brought down seven people , crashes his car into 3 other ones
    sends atruck in a plane tree and ends up smashing the shop window of pump
    attendant.
    Three days after he opens an eye. He is in a bed at the hospital , sees a
    doctor leaning over him
    _Well doctor ?
    _Well, I got the results : there is little blood in your alcohool.

19 :
    A truck driver in a state of total collapse reports to the police
    station :
    - Do you have black cows around here ?
    _ No
    _ Black horses?
    _ No
    _ And what about big black dogs?
    _ No
    _Then, I ran over the priest.

45:
    A warrant officer rassemble the section and announces:
    "Next Sunday there will be the Victory Parade . If it rains in the morning
    it will take place in the afternoon, and if it rains in the afternoon it
    will take place in the morning. "

64:
    A soldier complains to the warrant officer in charge of the intendance
    _Sir, THey served us duck paté at the canteen, and I can swear there was
    not any bit of duck in it .
    _So what! replies the warrant officer . Have you ever eaten soldier _
cookies?
    _Well ...Yes Sir
    _And did find any soldiers in it?

Two women are complaining about their boyfriends. One says to the
other, "Oh God, here comes a delivery man with a bunch of roses.
Christ, now I'll have to spend the entire weekend flat on my back
with my legs spread in the air." The other woman says, "Why don't
you just put them in a vase?"

HELVITICA BOLD please

I took another girl home ... I told her I'd like to see what her
apartment looked like. She drew me a sketch.

OUR FAX IS

233 2726.
                    FAX
CAN YOU SEND ME

WHAT YOU ALREADY

MADE AND DO THE

ABOVE JUICE AS WELL

WHEN YOU CAN

Thanks.   S.

I took another girl home from a date... I told her I'd like to
see what her apartment lookied like. She drew me a sketch.

I took another girl home from a date ... I tod her I'd like to

"He asked me about some of my lovers. That didn't bother me, and I asked him about some
of his lovers. What *did* bother me was that some of my lovers were some of his lovers."

"He asked me about some of my lovers. That didn't bother me,
and I asked him about some of his lovers. What *did* bother me
was that some of my lovers were some of his lovers."

Go ahead, make me gay!

Go ahead make me gay!

I walked into a stationery store and asked for a nice pen.
The clerk said, "A suprise?"
I said, "It will be. My wife's expecting a car!"

A doctor examined a woman and told her husband, "I'm not too
thrilled with your wife's looks."
The husband said, "That makes two of us!"

A doctor examined a woman and told her husband, "I'm not too
thrilled with your wife's looks."
I said "Hey Doc. No shit."

A young black kid bragged to the judge that he'd shot another
kid for a quarter. The judge said, "How can you shoot somebody
for a quarter?"
The kid replied, "You know how it is, Judge. Two bits here,
two bits there- it adds up!"

I was so ugly, when I was born the doctor slapped himself.

I was so ugly, when I was born the doctor slapped my mother.

She was so ugly, when she was born the doctor slapped her mother.

A man comes home and finds his best friend in bed with his wife.
The man throws up his hands in disbelief and says, "Rick, I have
to, but you?" *but you too?"*

Ninety percent of accidents occur in the kitchen. And my wife
cooked quite a few of them!

Did you know that nine out of ten accidents occur in the kitchen?
No shit, my wife she cooks three of them a day.

Hey thanks very much you've been great. Great!

What did I know? Until I was sixteen, I thought my sister
was a soft boy!

She's so hairy she doesn't need a coat. She is a coat!

He's so hairy he doesn't need a coat. He is a coat!

Hey Thanks very much.
No shit.

With the cost of funerals today, going down is going up.

I stumbled upon a funeral. By the time the minister, rabbi,
priest got through telling how comfortable the deceased was,
I wanted to be dead. *Too.*

She was so ugly, when she was born the doctor slapped himself.

Hey thanks very much.

I was an unloved baby. When I was missing, my folks tried to get my face off milk cartons.

He was an unloved baby. When he was missing, his folks tried to get his face off milk cartons.

A beggar walked up to me in the street and said, "I haven't had food in so long I've forgotten what it tastes like."
I said, "Don't worry. It still tastes the same."

A beggar walked up to me in the street and said, "I haven't had food in so long I've forgotten what it tastes like."
I said, "Hey, don't worry. It still tastes the same."

A beggar walked up to a man in the street and said, "I haven't had food in so long I've forgotten what it tastes like."
The man said, "Don't worry. It still tastes the same."

His folks kept him in a closet for years. Until he was fifteen, he thought he was a suit.

My parents had a real strange attitude about me. You could call it queer.

I'd rather die than wear a condom.

"My parents were strange. They kept me in a closet for years.
Until I was fifteen, I thought I was a suit."

"Did you know that nine out of ten accidents occur in the
kitchen?"
"No kidding, my wife she cooks three of them a day."

"Five years ago my wife ordered me to quit smoking and boozing."
"Did it work?"
"I don't know. I haven't seen her in five years."

A beggar walked up to me in the street and said, "I haven't
had food in so long I've forgotten what it tastes like."
I said, "Hey, don't worry. It still tastes the same."

A young black kid bragged to the judge that he'd shot another
kid for a quarter. The judge said, "How can you shoot somebody
for a quarter?"
The kid replied, "You know how it is, Judge. Two bits here,
two bits there- it adds up!"

I was so ugly, when I was born the doctor slapped my mother.

BADGEWORK

(23)

Henry, walking out of a house of questionable
repute, muttered to himself:
"Man, that's what I call a business....
You got it, you sell it, and you still got it."

Naughtical A petite young miss was discovered stowing away
in a lifeboat (a day after a liner left New York)
The captain ordered her (sent) to his cabin. "I don't
know what to do with you." he roared (after
questioning her.
"Say, skipper," she asked (finally), "How long
have you been a sailor?"

The worried woman (man) finally entered the
psychiatrist's office. He asked her to lie
on the couch, and said:
"Tell me, how did your trouble start?"
"This way."

The traveling salesman's car broke down one
evening on a lonely road, and he asked at
the only farmhouse in sight, "Can put me
up for the night?"
"I reckon I can," said the farmer, "but
you'll have to share a room with my young son."
"How about that!" gasped the salesman. "I'm in the wrong joke!"

Man walking out of a house of questionable repute, muttered to himself, "Man, that's what I call a business...you got it, you sell it, and you still got it."

Male Patient to Lady Psychiatrist: "I had a dream about you last nite." "Did you?" asked the Lady Doc. "No you wouldn't let me."

Two women are complaining
about their boyfriends. One
says to the other, "Oh God, here
comes a delivery man with a
bunch of roses. Christ, now I'll
have to spend the entire weekend
flat on my back with my legs
spread in the air." The other woman
says, "Why don't you just put
them in a vase?"

Man walking out of a house of
questionable repute, muttered to
himself, "Man, that's what I call
a business...you got it, you sell it,
and you still got it."

Male Patient to Lady Psychiatrist:
"I had a dream about you last
nite." "Did you?" asked the
Lady Doc. "No you wouldn't
let me."

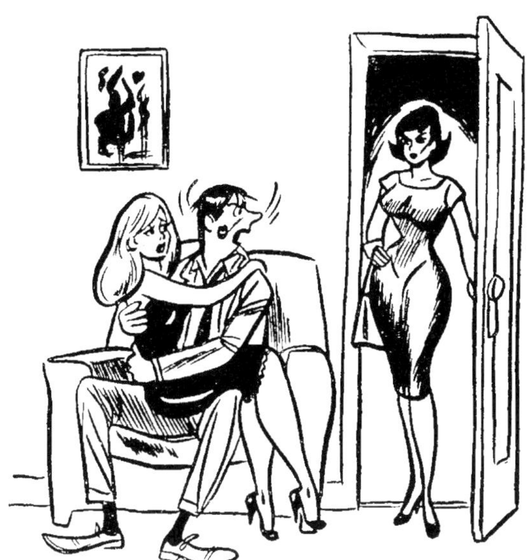

More Bird Talk

Opus Jocti Fiorentini: better known as Giotto.

My boyfriend just married a girl who was bi-sexual. Claimed he was going
to change her. He did. Three years later she's a lesbian.

On New Year's Day in 1929, a lonely frightened girl boarded a train for
Hollywood. She clutched a telegram in one hand and a small suitcase in the
other. The telegram read: Lucille Lesueur you have been placed under
contract, stop, MGM studios, stop, six months option, stop….
The above from a portrait of Joan, an autobiography by Joan Crawford with
Jane Kesner, 1962, Doubleday & Co., Garden City, New York.

In non-violence the bravery consists in dying, not killing.

In the dictionary of Satyagraha, there is no enemy.

Some people try to control the weather by blowing up the moon.

Lobbying means spending money.

A week wait for a gun.

Safe and sound.

The little guy behind the screen. The wizard of Oz. Is that what artist's are?
Little people behind the screen?

There's always one bad apple in the barrel. So what do you do? Get rid of
the barrel?

Why do some people want to stand out. To be different…

Sometimes when the phone rings, late at nite, I think… that's my wife
calling. Then I think, I'm not married anymore.

Goya's "Woman With A Fan", freedom of brushwork, the velvet depth of
the black and greasy, the simlifications of forms have a curiously modern
accent, which anticipated Monet.

A boy and his father are having dinner
in a Chinese restaurant. The boy asks
his father, "Is there such a thing
as 'Chinese Jews'?" His father replies,
"I don't know, son, why don't we ask the
Chinese waiter."
So they ask the waiter + he replies,
"No, but we have apple juice and orange juice."

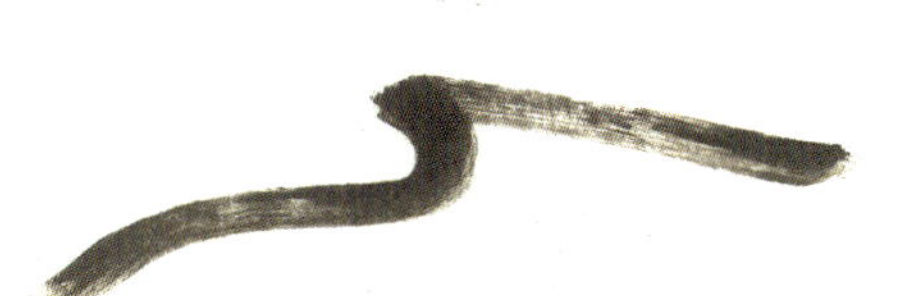

I said to my Mother-in-law, "My house is your house".
Last week she sold it.

While playing golf today, I hit two good balls.
I stepped on a rake.

I just heard from Bill Bailey. He's not coming home.

I was a pretty good fighter. I won my first
few fights, then I ran into trouble. They made me
fight a man.

My best punch was a rabbit punch, but they wouldnt
let me fight a rabbit.

What a fight. When the bell rang, I came
out of my corner and threw six straight punches in a row.
Then the other guy came out of his corner.

My wife is always asking for money.
$200 one day, 150 the next, $125 after that.
"Thats crazy" my friend said, "what does she do with it all?"
"I dont know" I said " I never gave her any".

A guy calls me up and says "What time does the
show go on?" I says, "What time can you make it?"

Every time I meet a girl who can cook like my
Mother... She looks like my Father.

My wife went to the beauty shop and got
a mud pack. For two days she looked beautiful.
Then the mud fell off.

Ive been married for thirty years and Im still
in love with the same woman. If my wife ever finds
out, she'll kill me

A husband comes home with a half-gallon of ice cream and asks his
   wife if she wants some.
   "How hard is it?" she asks.
   "About as hard as my dick." he replies.
   "Ok, then pour me some!"

I WAS A pretty good fighter
I won my FIRST FEW FIGHTS
THEN THEY MADE ME FIGHT
A MAN

Ladies and Gentlemen.
A funny thing happened to me while coming out to the microphone. I forgot my act.

I won't say what she does for a living but they threw her out of one hotel cause she didn't have a permit for a parade.

I once gave my girlfriend an old swimming suit, with the covered knees and long skirt and made out of corduroy. She was just delighted with it- laughing, skipping, running around whirring up a storm. Then she jumped in the water and we never saw her again.

I won't say she's fat, but who else has trouble getting into a bathrobe.

Rick's bisexual.. any time he wants it he has to buy it.

I collect rare photographs- I got one where Norman Rockwell is beating up a child.

I got some powdered water, but I don't know what to add.

What's the difference between a penis and a bonus? You can always get your wife to blow your bonus.

A guy goes to the doctor and says..Doc I got this terrible case of discolored penis. Sure enough the guy shows the Doc a bright blazing orange penis. The Doc had never seen anything quite like it and starts asking about the guy's daily routine. .. Any prescription medicine, did he have more intercourse than average, did he play any unusual athletics ?? Nope says the guy. About the only thing I do anymore is lay around eating Cheetos and watch the playboy channel.

I put an ad in the classifieds: "Wife Wanted". The next day I got a hundred replies. They all said the same thing.. You can have mine.

"Doctor, my husband limps because his left leg is an inch shorter than his right. What would you do in his case ?"
"Probably limp."

With all I've heard about A-bombs that'll destroy a city and H-bombs that'll destroy a state and chain reactions that'll destroy the world... you know I just don't have any incentive to buy a two pants suit.

What a kid I was. I remember practicing the violin in front of a roaring fire. My old man walked in. He was furious. We didn't have a fireplace.

With all I've heard about A-bombs

that'll destroy a city and H-bombs

that'll destroy a state and chain

reactions that'll destroy the world

you know I just havn't any incentive

to buy a two pants suit.

There's a guy who has a new cat. This cat he falls in love with. The cat falls in love with this guy. They're crazy about each other. Then this guy wins a free trip to Paris. So he leaves the cat with his sister.

Two weeks later he calls the sister from Paris. Over the phone he says, "How's my cat?" The sister says, "Your cat died."

He says, "Why did you tell it to me that way? You could have told me the cat was on the roof, fell off, broke its leg... you know, you could have told me gradually."

The sister says, "I'm sorry."

"She's on the roof."

The mother took her incorrigible son to the
psychiatrist. "Does he seem to feel insecure?"
asked the doctor. "No," the mother replied, "but
everyone else in the neighborhood does."

Three doctors were given six months to live. They
were told they could have anything they wanted.
The first doctor was a Frenchman. He wanted a beautiful
villa on the Riviera, surrounded by gorgeous young girls.
The second doctor was an Englishman, and he wanted
to have tea with the Queen. The third doctor was
Jewish. He wanted the opinion of another doctor.

I placed an ad in a swingers magazine
and my parents answered it.

My mother and father keep fighting. They rant and
they rave and they shout.
"Who is your father?" somebody asked.
"That's what they're fighting about."

The mother took her incorrigible son to the
psychiatrist. "Does he seem to feel insecure?"
asked the doctor. "No," the mother replied, "but
everyone else in the neighborhood does."

Three doctors were given six months to live. They
were told they could have anything they wanted.
The first doctor was a Frenchman. He wanted a beautiful
villa on the Riviera, surrounded by gorgeous young girls.
The second doctor was an Englishman, and he wanted
to have tea with the Queen. The third doctor was
Jewish. He wanted the opinion of another doctor.

I placed an ad in a swingers magazine
and my parents answered it.

My mother and father keep fighting. They rant and
they rave and they shout.
"Who is your father?" somebody asked.
"That's what they're fighting about."

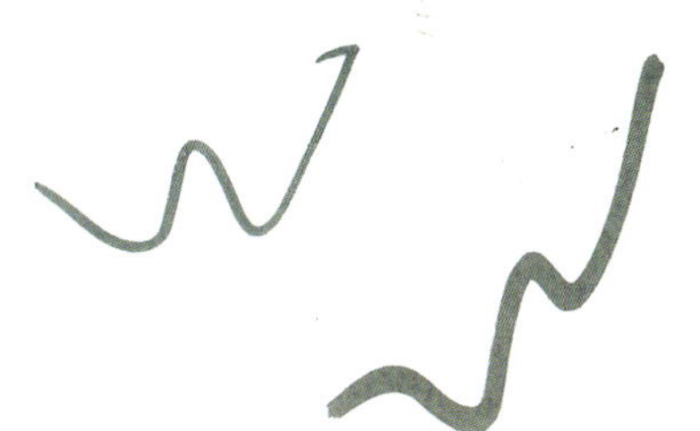

RICHARD PRINCE – JOKES

I said to my mother- in- law, "My house is your house".
Last week she sold it.

While playing golf today, I hit two good balls.
I stepped on a rake.

I just heard from Bill Bailey. He's not coming home.

I was a pretty good fighter. I won my first few fights, then I ran into trouble.
They made me fight a man.

My best punch was a rabbit punch,
But they wouldn't let me fight a rabbit.

What a fight. When the bell rang, I came out of my corner and threw six straight
Punches in a row. Then the other guy came out of his corner.

My wife is always asking for money.
$200 one day, $150 the next, $125 after that.
"That's crazy" my friend said, "what does she do with it all?"
"I don't know" I said, "I never gave her any".

A guy calls me up and says, "what time does the show go on?"
 I says, "what time can you make it?"

Every time I meet a girl who can cook like my
Mother…she looks like my father.

My wife went to the beauty shop and got a mud pack.
For two days she looked beautiful.
Then the mud fell off.

A wife went in to see a therapist and said, "I've got a big problem doctor"
Every time we're in bed and my husband climaxes, he lets out this
earsplitting yell."

"MY dear," the shrink said, "that's completely natural. I don't see what
problem is?"

"The problem is," she complained, "It wakes me up."

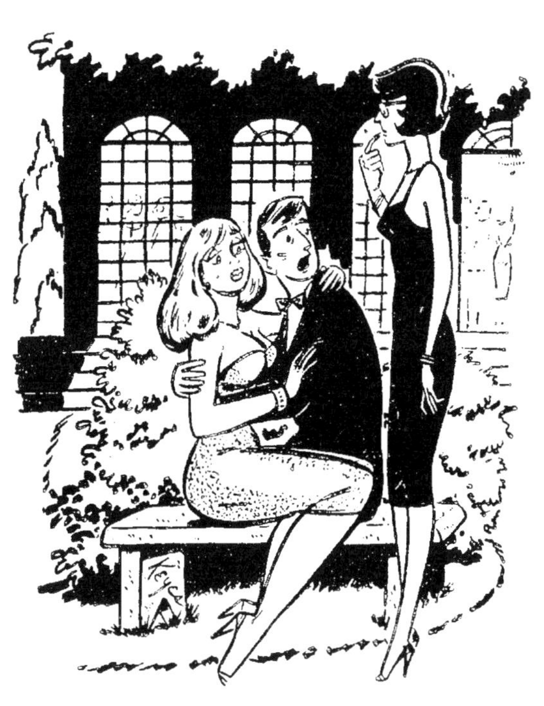

A housewife xxx selected three small tomatoes and was told by the grocer they
were 75 cents. "What!" she exclaimed, "&5 cents for those small tamatoes?
Well, you can just take them and you know what you can do with them!"
"I can't lady," replied the unhappy grocer, "there's a 95 cent cucumber there."

An inmate of the lunatic asylum was to be examined for dismissal. The first
question asked was: "What are you gonig to do when you get out of here?"
The inmate repled: I'm going going to get me a sling shot and come come back back
and break every damn window in the place!"
    After six months in his padded cell, he was was again questioned.
    'Well, I'm going to get a job," was the reply.
    "Fine," said the examiner. "And then what?"
    "Then I'm going to buy a big car."
    "Good"
    "And then, I'm going to meet a beautiful girl."
    "That's wonderful."
    "Then I'm going to take her out driving on a lonely road."
    "Yes"
    "Then I'm going to grab her garter belt, make a sling shot, and come back
here and break every window in the place."

    The good doctor had been an inspiration to the jungle natives. He had cured
their sick and taught them the religious and moral values of his won England.
He was loved and respected by every native in the village, but on this this
particular afternoon the chief was obviously troubled as he entered the doctor's
hut.
    "You live among my people long time now," said the chief. "You tell us not
right for man and girl to be close together before a marriage and we believe
what you say. This morning white child born to woman in village. You only white
man in jungle. What I tell my people?"
    The doctor smiled and led the chief to a window. "My son," he said, " I won't
attempt to give you a full scientific scientific explanation for the phenomenon known
as an albino. But look at the flock of sheep upon that hill hill. Every one is
snow white excet one. The white baby born to the woman in your village means
nothing more or less than that one black sheep in the white flock. It is simply
one of nature's mysterious accidents accidents."
    The black chief became embarrassed and looked at his feet. "OK, doc,"
he said. "You no tell- I no tell."

some people would try to control the weather by
blowing up the moon.

keep your thoughts to yourself.
Tying the knot.
Lobbying means spending money

CANDY stripe
Candy stripe?

So many things or at least
the reaction to things is based
on your mood

a week wait for a gun

safe and no sound
should I buy a gun? Yes.

The little guy behind the screen
the wizard of oz. Is that what
artists are? Little people behind
screens.

There always is one, at least one bad
apple in the barrel. So what do you
do, get rid of the barrel.

why do some people want to stand out? Be different?

Sometimes when the phone rings, late at nite, I think...that's
my wife calling, then I realize, I'm not married anymore.

Drinking yourself to death.

"Opus Joёti Fiorentini" better known as Giotto.

Mona Lisa was Mona Lisa del Giocondo whose portrait was painted at Florence 1503-1507

Hennrickje Stoffels, rembrant's servant, faithful and devoted companion, model for "Bathsheba", not a beautiful but impressively grandeur body

Rubens "Disembarkation of Marie de Médicis at Marseille" one of 26 paintings commissioned by Marie de Médicis for he palace of the Luxembourg at Paris.

Goya's "Woman with a Fan", freedom of brushwork. The velvet depth of the blacks and greys, or the simplification of the forms have a curiously modern accent, which anticipated Monet.

Jacopo Robusti, better known as Tintoretto (1518-94)

Paolo Caliari, known as Veronese, who was born at Verona as his pseudonym indicates.

evocative atmosphere, Arcadian poetry, mystery, music and melancholy, captivating color, revolutionary chandes by Giorgione at Venice.

4

Three doctors were given six months to live.
They were told they could have anything they wanted.
The first doctor was a Frenchman.
He wanted a beautiful villa on the Riviera, surrounded by gorgeous young girls.
The second doctor was an Englishman, and he wanted to have tea with the queen.
The third doctor was Jewish. He wanted the opinion of another doctor.

I placed an add in a swingers magazine and my parents answered it.

The mother took her incorrigible son to the psychiatrist.
"Does he seam to feel insecure?" asked the doctor,
"No" the mother replied, "but everyone else in the neighborhood does".

A man takes a girl to the Chatterbox hotel.
 Upon arrival the man says to the girl:
I'm gonna make love to you like you've never been loved before.
An hour latter the girl runs a pillow feather over the mans forehead.
The man pipes up: "Hey what do you think your doing?"
The girl replies: "comparatively speaking, I'm beating your brains out".

My father used to talk to me, he'd say, "listen, stupid,"-he always called me "listen".

I called down to the desk. I said, "Is this room service?"
She said, "yes". I said "Send up a room".

The ideal wife would be a beautiful, sex starved, deaf mute who owns a liquor store.

A pan handler said to me, "Mister, I haven't tasted food for a week."
I said, "Don't worry, it still tastes the same."

Why did Jesus cross the road? Because he was nailed to the chicken.

① I went to see a psychiatrist. He said, "Tell me everything." I did, and now he's doing my act.

② I NEVER HAD A PENNY TO MY NAME. So I CHANGED MY NAME.

Fireman pulling DRUNK out of a burning bed: "You darned fool, that'll teach you to smoke in bed."

③ DRUNK: "I WASN'T SMOKING IN bed, it WAS on fire when I laid DOWN."

④ WHAT A KID I WAS. I remember practicing the violin in front of a roaring fire. My old man walked in. He was furious. We didn't have a fireplace

⑤ A TRAVELING salesman's CAR broke DOWN ON a lonely road late at Nite in the middle of nowhere. He walked to the Nearest farmhouse and asked the farmer if he could stay the NIGHT. "No," said the farmer AND THEN SHOT the salesman in the head with a shotgun.

⑥ I'm always kidding about. My wife says the bartender. "Everytime I introduce her to anybody they say. "Are you kidding."

⑦ TWO FRIENDS RAN into each other at the door of a psychiatrist's office. "Are you coming or going?" asked one. The other replied, "If I knew, I wouldn't be here."

I never had a penny to my name, so x I changed my name.

K Fireman pulling drunk out of a burning bed: "You darned fool, that'll
teach you to smoke in bed."
  Drunk: "I wasn't smoking in bed, it was on fire when I laid down."

I eat politics and I sleep politics, but I never drink politics.

Here's my life story. I came from a very poor family. They couldn't
afford m to have children, so our neighbor had me.
X
I met my first girl, her name was Sally. Was that a girl... was that a
girl. XXXXX That's xxxxxxxx what people kept asking.

I went to see a phx psychiatrist. He said "Tell me everything." I did,
and now he's doing my act.

My father was never home, he was always away drinking booze. He saw a sign
saying DRINK CANADA DRY. So he went up there.

The way xxxxxxx she looks in the morning! She xxx ran after the garbage
man and said, "Am I too late for the xxxxxx garbage?" He said, "No,
jump in."

A traveling salesman's car broke down one evening on a lonely road and he
asked at the only farmhouse in sight, "Can you put me up for the night?"
"I reckon I can," said the farmer, "but you'll have to share a room with my
young son." "How about that," gasped the salesman, "I'm in the wrong joke."

"Are you drinking again? Doesn't your health mean xxxxxxxx anything to you?"
"Yes, it means something to drink to."

Two friends ran into each other at the door of a psychiatrist's office.
"Are you coming or going?" said one. The other xxxxxx replied, "If I knew
I wouldn't be here."

The old man stood at the gates of the cemetery and wept. A passer-by stopped
to comfort him. "Why are you crying?" the latter askdd softly. "My daughter
is laying in there," explained the weeping one. "Sometimes I wish she was dead."

A pink elephant, a green knagaroo and two yellow snakes strolled up to a xxx bar.
"You're here a little early, boys," said the bartender, "He ain't here yet."

MY neighbor's wife cried to me: "It was driving me crazy," she xxx said, "I
didn't know where he spent his evenings. One night I went xxx home, and there
he was."

Nancy to her girlfriend: "He said he was interested in humiliation, so I stood
him up."

"Im always kidding about my wife," says the xxxx bartender, "Everytime I intoduce
her to anybody, they d say, "Are you kidding?"

"Ich habe Pech bei den Frauen", seufzt Karl-Egon. "Gestern
war ich mit Lisa in einem Restaurant. Sie fand eine Raupe
auf ihrem Salat, rief den Kellner und sagte: 'Herr Ober,
entfernen Sie sofort dieses Untier!'
Da packte mich der Kellner und setzte mich vor die Tür!"

One guy telling another about his bad luck with women.he
has been in a restaurant with a gal who has been very disgusted at a maggot in her meal, demanding the waiter to
take it away. Instead doing this the waiter kicked the guy
out of the restaurant.

Anruf bei der Polizei: "In meinem Zimmer tickt eine
Bombe. Was soll ich machen?"
"Wir kommen. Solange sie tickt, haben Sie nichts zu
befürchten."

Someone is calling the police, declaring that there is
a bomb ticking in his room. Police is replying that
there is nothing to fear as long as the bomb is ticking.

Sie schluchzt: "Du hast das Versprechen nicht gehalten,
das du mir gegeben hast!"
"Weine nicht, Liebling, du kannst sofort ein neues haben."

Woman sighing because her lover did not keep his promise.
He is telling her that he might make a new one to her
immediately.

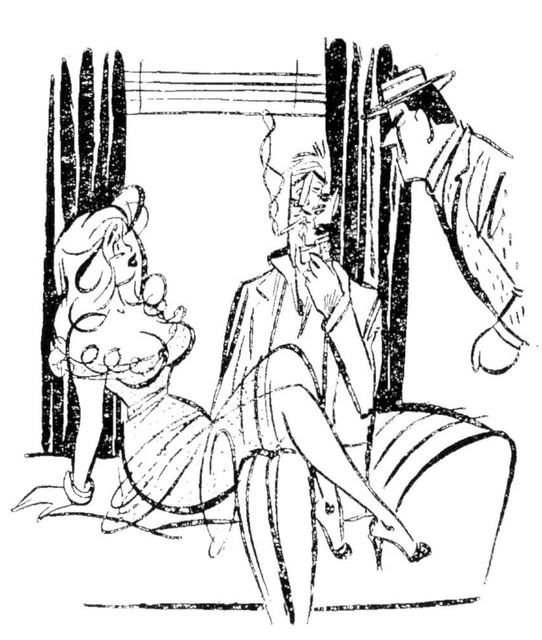

I waited on the corner for my blind date. When this girl walked by I said, "Are you Linda?" She said, "Are you Richard?" I said "Yeah." She said, "I'm not Linda."

A man's watch breaks. He walks down a street and spots a store with an enormous watch hanging in the window. The man behind the counter tells him, "Sorry, I don't fix watches, I perform circumcisions."
"Circumcisions?" cries the man with the broken watch. "Then what's with the large watch hanging in the window?"
"Mister, what do you suggest I hang in the window?"

Two men go on a hunting trip. One of them is attacked by a poisonous snake which bites him on the penis. He is in excrutiating pain, and his friend runs to the nearest town to find a doctor. he describes the injury to the doctor, and the doctor tells him to go back immediately and put his mouth over the wound, draw out the poison, and spit it out. That's the only hope for saving his friend's life.
The man goes back to his injured friend, who is yelping in pain. "What did the doc say?" he asks from between gritted teeth.
"He says you're going to die."

I don't like to brag but I got good-looking kids. thank god my wife cheated on me.

A long-haired hippie was hitchhiking when a trucker picked him up. Heading down the road, the hippie says to the trucker, "Bet you thought I was a girl."
Replies the trucker, "Don't matter much, was gonna fuck ya anyway."

White man: "I don't know what to do. My house has burned to the ground, my wife died, mycar's been stolen, and the doctor says I gotta have a serious operation."
Black man: "What you kickin' about, you white ain't you?"

A Russian man saves up enough money to by a refrigerator. he goes to the appropriate office and hands over the money.
"Your refrigerator," the official tells him, "will be delivered exactly ten years from today."
"In the morning or in the afternoon?" the man asks.
"Why do you need to know that now?" the official asks.
"Because the plumber promised to come in the morning."

An American, a Pole, a Chinaman, and an Israeli are standing on a street corner when a man comes over with a clipboard.
"Excuse me," he says. "I am taking a poll. What is your opinion of the meat shortage?"
The American asks: "What's a 'shortage'?"
The Pole asks: "What's 'meat'?"
The Chinaman asks: "What's an 'opinion'?"
The Israeli asks: "What's 'excuse me'?"

I grew up to have my father's looks, my father's speech patterns, my father's posture, my father's opinions and my mother's contempt for my father.

How do we know Jesus was Jewish?
1. He was thirty, unmarried, and still living with his mother.
2. He went into his father's business.
3. He thought his mother was a virgin.
4. And his mother thought he was god.

A mother is having a very tense relationship with her fourteen year old son. Screaming and fighting are constantly going on in the house. She finally brings him to a psychoanalyst. After two sessions, the doctor calls the mother into the office.
"Your son," he tells her, "has an Oedipus complex."
"Oedipus, Scmedipus," the woman answers. "As long as he loves his mother."

Samplings

No more one thing at a time.

I placed an ad in a swingers magazine, and my parents answered it.
Men and woman.
Men and men.
Woman and woman.

The line we strive for. A smooth curve over the hips.

We're stoned. What are you going to do about it?

Woobie: a mello bozo.

We will not go back.

Do you know what it means to come home at night to a woman who'll give you a little love, a little affection, a little tenderness? It means your're in the wrong house, that's wht it means.

Anyone can find me.

What we want is a roomfull of people where everyone is sexy and everyone is powerful.

Between the ages of 14 and 17 I saw "Enter The Dragon" 22 times before I stopped counting.

No glove, no love.

She sells beer, she sells cigarettes and clothes; every nite she's on t.v. Every week she's on every other page of the magazines and at the movies too. There she is.

I wanna be your dog.

In the 16 year old's room: Army packs, smoke grenades, ammunition pouches, four shotguns, a revolver, Rambo posters and magazines.

~~SAMPLINGS   SAMPLINGS~~

Sammy's "Why Me?"... the sequel to his "Yes I Can".

yo yo: somewhere between a squid and a klutz.

Colombian "cartels", Asian "triads and tongs", Jamaican "posses".

"Embraceable You" (1948) Dane Clark. Geraldine Brooks. Crook loves hit-and-run victim.

The Koran makes it clear: if someone defames the Prophet, then he must die.

Photography reached Africa on Nov. 6, 1879

An eight-year-old hadn't said one word in his entire life. One day, however, as the family sat down to have breakfast, the boy asked, "Do we have any jam?"

The family was stunned. When they'd recovered, his father said, "How come you never said one word before?"

The boy said, "Well, up until now, everything's been okay!"

A husband was telling a friend, "If my wife really loved me, she would have married somebody else!"

My wife said, "If you really had loved me, you would have married somebody else!"

My brother is an inconsiderate husband. He won a trip for two to Paris. He went twice!

I guess I was a pretty inconsiderate husband. I won a trip for two to Paris. So I went twice.

A long-haired hippie was hitchhiking when a ~~trucker~~
Trucker picked him up. ~~Climb~~ ~~Climbing into the~~
cab of the ~~truck~~ ~~After traveling.~~
Heading down the ~~road~~ the hippie says to the
Trucker "Bet you thought I was a girl.
Replies the Trucker — Don't matter much
was ~~goin to to to~~ gonna fuck ya anyway.

An eighty-three-year-old man comes into the confessional. "Father," he says. "I must speak to you. I am a widower, and very lonely. Last week, though, I met a beautiful twenty-six-year-old

girl. She really liked me. I took her to a hotel, and in the last five days, I've made love to her fourteen times."

"You should say ten Hail Marys," the priest tells him.

"Why should I do that? I'm Jewish, Father."

"Jewish? Then why are you telling me this?"

"Telling you? I'm telling everybody."

A man's watch breaks. He walks down a street spots a stone with an enormous watch hanging in the window. The man behind the counter tells him "sorry" "I Don't fix watches, I perform circumcisions."

"Circumcisions?" cries the man with the broken watch. Then what's with the large watch hanging in the window?

"Mister, what Do you suggest I hang in my window?"

Two men go on a hunting trip. One of them is attacked by a poisonous snake, which bites him on the penis. He is in excruciating pain, and his friend runs to the nearest town to find a doctor. He describes the injury to the doctor, and the doctor tells him to go back immediately and put his mouth over the wound, draw out the poison, and spit it out. That's the only hope for saving his friend's life.

The man goes back to his injured friend, who is yelping in pain. "What did the doc say?" he asks from between gritted teeth.

"He said you're going to die."

a friend of mine survives

White man: "I don't know what to do, my house has burned to the ground, my wife died, my car's been stolen, and the doctor says I gotta have a serious operation."

Black man: "What you kickin' about, you white ain't you?"[14]

I never had a penny to my name, so I changed my name.

Nancy to her girlfriend: "He said he was interested in humiliation, so I stood him up."

"I'm always kidding about my wife," says the bartender. "Every time I introduce her to anybody, they say, 'Are you kidding?'"

"I eat politics and I sleep politics, but I never drink politics."

the way she looks in the morning! She ran after the garbage man and said, "Am I too late for the garbage?" He said, "No, jump in."

I went to see a psychiatrist. He said, "Tell me." I did, and now he's doing my act.

A husband was telling a friend, "If my wife really loved me, she would have married somebody else!"

My wife's a funny woman. All the time she's telling me:
My wife said, "If you really loved me, you would have married somebody else!"

My wife said, "If you really had loved me, you would have married somebody else!"

My brother was an inconsiderate husband. He won a trip for two to Paris. He went twice!

I guess I was a pretty inconsiderate husband. I won a trip for two to Paris. So I went twice.

Hey Thanks very much.

I'd like to share this honor with all the people who helped me. But since there aren't any, I won't.

My grandmother used to say, "In somebody else's bed you can't find happiness!" But you can come up with a lot of laughs.

The man comes home and finds his best friend in bed with his wife. The man throws up his hands in disbelief and says, "Rick, I have to, but you too?"

A man comes home and finds his best friend in bed with his wife.

7

My wife's a funny woman. All the time she's telling me;
"If you really loved me, you would have married somebody else!"

8

I guess I was a pretty inconsiderate husband. I won a trip
for two to Paris. So I went twice.

9

Hey Thanks very much.

10

A man comes home and finds his best friend in bed with his wife.
The man throws up his hands in disbelief and says, "Rick, I have
to, but you too?"

11

She's so hairy she doesn't need a coat. She is a coat!

12

I stumbled upon a funeral. By the time the minister, rabbi,
priest got through telling how comfortable the deceased was,
I wanted to be dead too.

13

One day a Greek insulted a Spaniard. The next morning, the
Germans declared war!

14

I'd rather die than wear a condom.
Mother. Brother. Sister. Father.

My parents kept me in a closet for years. Until I was fifteen,
I thought I was a suit.

She refused to go to bed with him because they weren't married.
So he married her. He carried her across the threshold. She took off
her lashes, her makeup, her padded bra, and her girdle. When
she was through, he respected her. He didn't recognise her,
but he respected her!

When I was a kid, they bought me a bat. I took it out in the
street to play with it, and it flew away!

One day a Greek insulted a Spaniard. The next morning, the
Germans declared war!

"Five years ago my wife ordered me to quit smoking and boozing."
"Did it work?"
"I don't know I haven't seen her in five years."

"Five years ago, when I was married, I ordered my husband to
quit smoking and boozing."
"Did it work?"
"I don't know. I haven't seen him in five years!"

I'd rather die than wear a condom.
Mother. Brother. Sister. Father.

Man walking out of a house of questionable repute, muttered to
himself, "Man, that's what I call a business...you got it, you
sell it, and you still got it."

Male Patient to Lady Psychiatrist: "I had a dream about you last
nite."Did you?" asked the Lady Doc. "No you wouldn't let me."

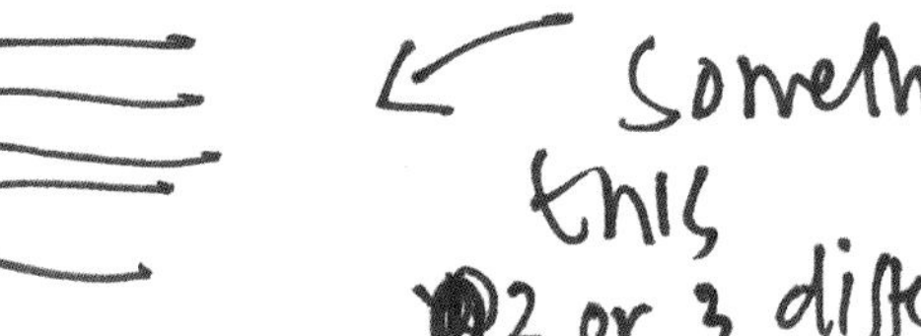

All usual Helvilica Bold

DEAR SST:
Can you do these in one line
① (each joke = on one line)

② and then as above

③ and then on shorter lines

doble le ________ ________ ← something like
                                this
                              2 or 3 different ways

17. I went to the doctor because I'd swallowed a bottle of sleeping pills.
My doctor told me to have a few drinks and get some rest.

18. With my old man I got no respect. I asked him, "How can I get my kite
in the air?"
He told me to run off a cliff.

19. Some dog I got. We call him Egypt because in every room he leaves a
pyramid.
His favorite bone is in my arm Last night he went on the paper four times
three of those times I was reading it.

20. One year they wanted to make me poster boy for birth control.

21. My uncle's dying wish was to have me sitting in his lap; he was in the
electric chair.

I'm so ugly; when I was born the doctor slapped my mother!

———————————— Headers ————————————
Return-Path: <jeffrey.rian@wanadoo.fr>
Received: from rly-xh06.mx.aol.com (rly-xh06.mail.aol.com [172.20.115.236]) by air-xh03.mail.aol.com (v97.18) with ESMTP
id MAILINXH31-71240100a8118b; Thu, 22 Jan 2004 12:38:44 -0500
Received: from mwinf0302.wanadoo.fr (smtp3.wanadoo.fr [193.252.22.28]) by rly-xh06.mx.aol.com (v97.10) with ESMTP id
MAILRELAYINXH68-71240100a8118b; Thu, 22 Jan 2004 12:38:10 -0500
Received: from [81.251.32.246] (ATuileries-117-1-36-246.w81-251.abo.wanadoo.fr [81.251.32.246])
    by mwinf0302.wanadoo.fr (SMTP Server) with ESMTP id 39F4BC000273
    for <Richardprin@aol.com>; Thu, 22 Jan 2004 18:38:09 +0100 (CET)
User-Agent: Microsoft-Outlook-Express-Macintosh-Edition/5.02.2106
Date: Thu, 22 Jan 2004 18:38:32 -0800
Subject: jokes
From: Jeff Rian <jeffrey.rian@wanadoo.fr>
To: Richard Prince <Richardprin@aol.com>
Message-ID: <BC35C928.91E%jeffrey.rian@wanadoo.fr>
Mime-version: 1.0
Content-type: text/plain; charset="ISO-8859-1"
Content-transfer-encoding: quoted-printable
X-AOL-IP: 193.252.22.28
X-AOL-SCOLL-SCORE: 0:XXX:XX
X-AOL-SCOLL-URL_COUNT: 0

    "If I refuse to go to bed with you"
She whispered,"will you really commit suicide?"
"That's been my usual procedure."

"I understand your husband drowned and left
you two million dollars. Can you imagine, two
million dollars, and he couldn't even read or write."
    "Yeah, she said, and he couldn't swim either."

Three doctors were given six months to live. They were told
they could have anything they wanted. The first doctor was a
Frenchman. He wanted a beautiful villa on the Riviera,
surrounded by gorgeous young girls. The second doctor was an
Englishman, and he wanted to have tea with the Queen. The third
doctor was Jewish. He wanted the opinion of another doctor.

Woman sighing because her lover did not keep his promise. He is
telling her that he might make a new one to her immediately.

One guy telling another about his bad luck with women. He has been
in a restaurant with a gal who has been very disgusted at a maggot
in her meal, demanding the waiter to take it away. Instead of doing
this the waiter kicked the guy out of the restaurant.

TWO LIONS SITTING AROUND AFTER SUPER: One lion says to the other,
"Hey, Sid, remember last summer when we were all gathered around
the kill and someone told a leopard joke, and you laughed so hard
an antler came out of your nose?"

George entered a bar and ordered a whisky sour and told the
bartender to fix the other guy at the bar a drink, too.
Finishing his first, he called to the bartender, "Fix me
another of the same but leave the fruit out of it."
"Hey man!" shrieked the other guy, "I didn't ask for a drink in
the first place!"

Do you know what it means to come home at night to a
woman who'll give you a little love, a little affection, a little
tenderness? It means you're in the wrong house, that's what.

Nancy to her girlfriend: "He said he was interested in humiliation,
so I stood him up."

An inmate of the lunatic asylum was to be examined
for dismissal. The first question asked was: "What are you going to
do when you get out of here?"
  The inmate replied: "I'm going to get me a sling shot and come
back and break every damn window in the place!"
  After six months in his padded cell, he was again questioned.
  "Well, I'm going to get a job," was his reply.
  "Fine," said the examiner. "And then what?"
  "Then I'm going to buy a big car."
  "Good."
  "And then, I'm going to meet a beautiful girl."
  "That's wonderful."
  "Then I'm going to take her out driving on a lonely road."
  "Yes"
  "Then I'm going to grab her garter, make a sling shot, and come
back here and break every window in the place."

GOOD NEWS BAD NEWS: A man walked into a doctor's office to get a
check-up. After the examination the doctor says to the man, I've
got good news and I've got bad news. The bad news is your going to
die in a year and there's nothing you can do about it. The good
news is I'm having an affair with my secretary.

What a kid I was. I remember practicing the violin in front of a
roaring fire. My old man walked in. He was furious. We didn't have
a fireplace.

Two girls meet on the beach at Miami. One says:
  "So what's new?"
  The other says," Wait'll you hear! I was at the doctor's
this morning, he gives me an examination, and you know what he
says? He says I'm gradually turning into a man."
  "So what else is new?"

With all I've heard about A-bombs that'll destroy a city and H-
bombs that'll destroy a state and chain reactions that'll destroy
the world... you know I just don't have any incentive to buy a two
pants suit.

Three doctors were given six months to live. They were told they could have anything they wanted. The first doctor was a Frenchman. He wanted a beautiful villa on the Riviera, surrounded by gorgeous young girls. The second doctor was an Englishman, and he wanted to have tea with the Queen. The third doctor was Jewish. He wanted the opinion of another doctor.

A man walked into a doctor's office to get a ceck-up. After the examination the doctor told him he had good news and he had bad news. The bad news was he was going to die in a year and there was nothing that could be done about it. The good news was that he was having an affair with his new secretary.

A man walked into a doctor's office to get a check-up. After the examination the Doctor said, "I've got good news and I've got bad news. The bad news is that your going to die in a year and there's nothing that can be done about it. The good news is that I'm having an affair with my new secretary.

A man walked into a doctor's office to get a check-up. After the examination the Doctor said, "I've got good news and I've got bad news. The bad news is that your going to die in a year and there's nothing that can be done about it. The good news is I'm having an affair with my secretary.

At a Mountaineer's cabin way up in the mountains a
very large family was seated around the dinner table
and, as customery, there was no passing of food. When
one wanted something, they just stood up reached for it
and some of the reaches were pretty long. One of the
older boys was sitting at the table and wanted a slice
of bread, so he stood up and reached far, far across the
table for it. The Father, sitting at the side, wrinkled
his brow and said, "Maw, how old is Zeke now?" and Maw
said, "Nigh on ta twenty, I recken". Paw very seriously
said, "Maw, it appears to me we better start putting pants
on Zeke. Did you see what he dragged through the soup?

The traveling salesman's car broke down one EVENING on a lonely road and he asked at the only farmhouse in sight " "Can you put me up for the night?" "I reckon I can," said the farmer, "but you'll have to share a room 'with my young son". How about that." ~~gasped~~ GASPED the SALESMAN, "I'm in the wrong 'joke"

RICHARD PRINCE

Jokes & Cartoons is based on the artist's contribution to the Ringier AG Annual Report 2005 and published on occasion of its realization. It was generously supported by Ringier AG, Corporate Communications, Zurich.

CONCEPT	Richard Prince	PUBLISHED BY	JRP|Ringier
			Letzigraben 134
EDITOR	Beatrix Ruf		CH-8047 Zurich
			T +41 (0) 43 311 27 50
COORDINATION	Myrta Bugini		F +41 (0) 43 311 27 51
			E info@jrp-ringier.com
GRAPHIC REALIZATION	Ines Häny, Schlumpf & Partner AG, Zurich		www.jrp-ringier.com
COLOR SEPARATION	Ringier, Specter, Zurich		ISBN 3-905701-83-9

CONCEPT — Richard Prince
EDITOR — Beatrix Ruf
COORDINATION — Myrta Bugini
GRAPHIC REALIZATION — Ines Häny, Schlumpf & Partner AG, Zurich
COLOR SEPARATION — Ringier, Specter, Zurich
PRINT — Zürcher Druck + Verlag AG, Rotkreuz
BINDING — Buchbinderei Burkhardt, Mönchaltorf
ACKNOWLEDGEMENTS — This publication has been made possible by Michael Ringier and Ringier AG, Corporate Communications, Zurich.
THANKS TO — Rosalie Benitez, Gilles Gavillet, Barbara Gladstone Gallery (New York)

PUBLISHED BY — JRP\|Ringier, Letzigraben 134, CH-8047 Zurich, T +41 (0) 43 311 27 50, F +41 (0) 43 311 27 51, E info@jrp-ringier.com, www.jrp-ringier.com

ISBN 3-905701-83-9

JRP\|Ringier books are available internationally at selected bookstores and the following distribution partners:

SWITZERLAND — Buch 2000, AVA Verlagsauslieferung AG, Centralweg 16, CH-8910 Affoltern a.A., buch2000@ava.ch, www.ava.ch

FRANCE — Les Presses du réel, 16 rue Quentin, F-21000 Dijon, info@lespressesdureel.com, www.lespressesdureel.com

GERMANY AND AUSTRIA — Vice Versa Vertrieb, Immanuelkirchstrasse 12, D-10405 Berlin, info@vice-versa-vertrieb.de, www.vice-versa-vertrieb.de

UK — Art Data, 12 Bell Industrial Estate, 50 Cunnington Street, UK-London W4 5 HB, info@artdata.co.uk, www. artdata.co.uk

USA — D.A.P./Distributed Art Publishers, l55 Sixth Avenue, 2nd Floor, New York, USA-NY 10013, dap@dapinc.com, www.artbook.com

OTHER COUNTRIES — IDEA Books, Nieuwe Herengracht 11, NL-1011 RK Amsterdam, idea@ideabooks.nl, www. ideabooks.nl

For a list of our partner bookshops or for any general questions, please contact JRP\|Ringier directly at info@jrp-ringier.com, or visit our homepage www.jrp-ringier.com for further information about our program.